Laughter with Today's Teenagers 101

By Nancy Burcham

Logan & Walker,
May you be blessed
with laughter,
Nancy Burcham

Love and Laughter ever after

to my husband, kids, kids-in law,

grandkids, grandkids-in-law,

and great-grandkids.

Table of Contents

For the glory of God.

Inspire kindness and respect.

Laughter Soothes the Soul

Laughter is magical.

It calms our beastly anger. For every minute we are angry, we lose 60 seconds of happiness, 60 seconds of joy. Laughter energizes us to bring the joy back into our lives.

It soothes our troubled souls. It's incredible that when we are laughing, we cannot feel anxious, worried or sad in our souls.

Laughter draws us closer to others at any stage or age in our lives. Nothing works faster to bring a connection between two people than a good kind laugh.

By looking for the humor in everyday life, we can view this enchanting world from a more relaxed, positive and joyful perspective. We can be kind, respectful and in tune with all ages, even today's teenagers --- especially today's teenagers.

Families and friends connect with one another when they learn to laugh at themselves. Consider texting.

Text from Dad to his teenage son Drew: Your mother and I are going to divorce next month.
Text from Drew: DAD? WHY? Call me!!!!!!
Text from Dad: Oh, this darn autocorrect. I wrote Disney and this phone changed it to divorce. We're going to Disney next month. Want to go?

Mom texting son Matthew: I've got something to tell you. Are you sitting down?
Son Matthew texting Mom: Actually, I am. What's up?
Mom: Your brother was adopted.

Matthew: WHAT? Why are you telling me this in a text? Call me!

Mom: It's this crazy phone! I wrote accepted and this phone changed it to adopted. Your brother was accepted at Yale.

To add to the baffling mix of today's technology, cell phones are so expensive that if you should fall and hear a cracking sound, you hope it's your leg and not the cell phone in your pocket.

Teens' texting relationship messages can really 'crack you up'. Try these out for a few chuckles.

Text from teenager David to friend Jackson: How is Ruth?

Jackson's return text: Not sure. I broke up with her last night.

David: Oh no, man. You re so Ruthless.

Jackson: How long have you been waiting to say that?

David: Just saying

Carrie texting to Classmate Lake: May I ask you some questions?

Lake: Ok???

Carrie: Please answer these 6 questions.

    1 What is your brother's name?

        2 Q,R,S,T,?

        3 What is the opposite of stop?

        4 What is the opposite of in?

        5 "I drank soda ? her"

        6 Can you spell me?

   Lake: 1 Will

       2 U

       3 go

       4 out

       5 with

       6 me

Carrie: YES!!!

Lake: What!!! Oh, I get it.

Rachel texting friend: Hey, why not come over tonight? We can talk about Nathan.

Return text: What about him?

Rachel texting: Hannah, you know we both like him. He's so hot!

Return text: Rachel???

Rachel: Yes?

Return text: Look who you're texting.

Rachel: OH! NATHAN. HI.

Nathan: LOL. Don't worry. I feel the same way about you

Tantalizing. That's what teenagers are. They tease our world with glimmers of maturity one moment, and revert to those childish ways the next. They dangle out false hope to entice us and make us believe they are finally exercising adult decisions, that they are thinking rationally and being responsible. Then, when they have the family car after a snowstorm, they take their friends for a ride, bury the car in three feet of snow, and call dear old dad to dig them out.

If, while looking with pride at his newborn child, a father was to somehow realize that in sixteen short years this tiny bundle of joy will be out joyriding in the family's latest car – and maybe bending a fender or two as teenagers sometimes do -- his joyful smile would surely fade into a concerned frown. It is a small blessing that he doesn't know this in advance. He has sixteen years to grow into becoming the father of a teenager behind the wheel.

Studies have shown that the teenage brain is still very much a work in progress and functions a 'bit' different than an adult's. Their hand/eye coordination and motor skills are as fine-tuned as they will ever be, but other skills like weighing priorities or consequences and planning ahead continue to develop into their 20s.

Our teenage son got his driver's license on the day he turned sixteen, and his driving record was accident-free for over two years. Then it happened. He did it, all by himself. On his way to pick up two girls and take them to a movie, he backed the family car out of the garage – almost, but not quite far enough.

The left front fender caught the side wall and pulled it off the foundation of the house.

The cracking noise was deafening.

His dad and I ran outside to see what had happened.

Our son was so angry at himself for doing such a careless thing and so busy calling himself dummy, stupid, and nitwit that his dad and I didn't have a chance to say anything as we examined the small dent in the front fender and the protruding wooden siding pulled away from the house frame work.

Our son finally turned to his dad and said, "How bad is it?"

Looking at the damaged house, his dad said, "I think that section needed new siding anyway. And son – the next time you plan a date, take only one girl at a time. Two girls must be more than you can handle."

His dad didn't yell at him and neither did I. I wanted to shout, "What were you thinking?" or "Why were you so careless?"

But I stopped myself just in the nick of time. Those questions were a waste of words.

They were questions to make my son feel worse than he already felt. And there was no sensible answer to an accident. That's why it's called an accident.

"I'm not going to the movie, Mom," our son said. "I'm too upset."

"Go ahead with your plans," I said. "What's done is done. Staying home isn't going to change anything. You'll just feel worse as the evening drags on."

After our son left, I asked my husband how he could remain so calm when I was seething inside. "Well," he said. "I took the time to remember my first accident when I was a teenager. After I got my license, I was leaving the driver's license place and backed into a car parked behind me. I'll never forget how awful I felt. I'm sure our son was feeling as bad if not worse."

Remembering how it felt to be a teenager and counting to ten before we spoke worked. They were two ways to help us show respect and choose kind words wisely.

Much later, our son said to us, "Your being nice to me was the hardest thing to take. I could only be angry at myself and not you two for yelling at me."

Today's teenagers live in a rapidly changing world, a world changing much faster than their parents or grandparents experienced growing up. Technology has virtually taken over the universe at a time when their brains are seeking a rewarding, happy life. In today's world of distracting smartphones, social media, and video games, they are trying to learn to plan ahead, consider consequences, and understand relationships.

We all need to connect without the use of technology.

Be in the moment. Take a deep breath. Pay attention.

Be happy now. We can't wait for someone else to make us happy. We have to simply determine to be happy, no matter what life throws at us. We need to learn that the greatest part of our happiness and laughter depends on our disposition and not our circumstances.

We can chose to be happy. Choose to be a kind example. Choose actions and attitudes that speak louder than words. Choose to look for the laughter in everyday life.

If someone says that getting a driver's license will not change a teenager, do not believe them. With her new driver's license in her pocket, Sarah and Tom's daughter Izzy changed overnight from being happy at home with Mom and Dad to a teenager who always 'needed the car' because she just had to go --- somewhere --- anywhere.

One day, she was a daughter who came in after school and said, "Hi, Mom. I'm glad I'm home."

The next day, she was sixteen, dashing through the house after school, rattling her keys. "I need the car," she said. "I *have* to go to Dollar General."

One day, she was a daughter who came in the kitchen and said, "Is there anything I can do to help with dinner?" The next day, she was sixteen, running through the house and saying, "I need the car keys right now. Beth and Jane are waiting for me. Oh, and don't fix me any dinner. We're going to meet friends for pizza --- if it's okay with you."

Tuesday morning was a surprising experience, one they weren't prepared for. But they will be when it happens again, which it surely will with teenagers in the house. Izzy sat down to breakfast and said, "Dad, why don't you take the car today?"

"Do you really mean it?" Her dad asked in an excited voice. "I can have the car at last? I don't have to walk to work in the rain?"

"Sure, why not." She said, getting up to leave. "Oh, by the way, Dad. You'll have to stop for gas on your way to work. The gauge is on empty."

That was a setting limits moment:

If you use the gas, replace the gas or you don't have car privileges.

Show respect with voice, words, deeds and following family curfews.

Be kind

We can choose kindness and laughter often. Start by not dwelling on the negative. Try to avoid negative people and don't watch too many news stories or anything that makes us sad and unhappy.

How do we show kindness?

Be helpful and care.

Be forgiving and forget.

Keep our promises.

Always tell the truth.

Say please, thank you, and excuse me.
Make eye contact.
Stand up straight and tall.
Listen to others. Be friendly. Be compassionate.
Respect others. Respect yourself.

Kindness is a creator of laughter. To find laughter, we should start with a smile, and look for the funny side of things. If we are upset over something we can ask ourselves, "How could this situation be funny?" Humor is a great way to deal with adversity. It can turn a negative into a positive.

If someone hurts your feelings or makes you angry, don't let them know your emotional response to their cruelty. Instead, kill them with kindness. They'll never know what hit them. Remember the golden rule: "Do unto others as you would have them do unto you".

Relax and be ready to laugh. Give yourself permission to be silly. In the right moment, being silly is a plus. Don't take yourself too seriously. Learn to laugh at your faults and your mistakes.

Try gently teasing others. Be sure to avoid meanness, rudeness, or anything that offends. Be a fine example. Carefully choose when and where to practice.

Create a joke jar in your home and encourage teenagers, kids and adults to contribute to it for shared laughter during dinner.

Here's a list of silly jokes to get you started.

Patient: "Doctor! Doctor! You have to help me! Some mornings I wake up and think I'm Donald Duck. Other mornings I think I'm Mickey Mouse."

Doctor: "Hmm, how long have you been having these Disney spells?"

A man on a plane stood up and shouted, "HIJACK!"
All the passengers were suddenly scared.

Then, from the other end of the plane, a guy shouted back, "HI, JOHN!"

I have a dog named Curiosity.
I no longer have a cat.

Brook called the vet. "Can you help me?" She said. "My cat is so lethargic. She's just lying there, barely breathing. What can I do?"

"Do you have any gasoline in the garage?" asked the vet.

"Yes."

"Good. Take a little gas and place it on your cat's tongue."

"Okay."

Brook placed a little gas on her cat's tongue. Her cat immediately jumped up, ran around the room several times, climbed up the living room curtains, ran across the curtain rod and scurried down the other side. Then her cat fell down and died.

Brook called the vet and told him what happened.

"I was afraid of that," he said. "I'm sorry, but your cat just ran out of gas."

Did you hear about the monkeys who shared an Amazon account?
They were Prime mates.

A man was recovering from minor surgery when a nurse came in his room to check on him. "How are you feeling?" She asked.

"I'm okay," he said. "But I didn't like the four-letter word the doctor used during surgery."

"What did he say?" the nurse asked.

"Oops."

Did you hear about the actor who fell through the floorboards?

He was just going through a stage.

"EBay is so useless. I tried to look up lighters and all they had were 2,996 matches."

The number 19 and 20 got into a fight. 21.

What did the bald man say when he got a comb for a present?

"Thanks --- I'll never part with it."

What did the buffalo say when his son left for college?

"Bison."

"What does the word contemplate mean?" The teenager asked his English teacher.

"Think about it," his teacher said.

"Geez," the student groaned. "Can't you just tell me?"

What's the best thing about Switzerland?

"I don't know but the flag is a huge plus."

What did the right eye say to the left eye?

"Between you and me, something smells."

On a frosty winter morning, Matt texted his wife Joni: "Windows frozen!"

Wife Joni texted back: "Pour lukewarm water on it."

Five minutes later, Matt replied: "Computer's completely messed up now."

Why was 2019 afraid of 2020?

Because they had a fight and 2021.

What do you call a parade line of rabbits hopping backwards?
A receding hare-line.

I recently got rid of my vacuum cleaner.
It was just gathering dust.

What kind of exercise do lazy people do?
Diddly-squats.

A man was on trial for armed robbery. When the jury came back with a verdict, the foreman stood and said, "Not Guilty."
"Awesome!" The man on trial shouted, jumping to his feet, "Do I get to keep the money?"

Kind laughter takes you to a higher place where you can view the world with a more peaceful, optimistic, and joyful attitude.
Don't take yourself too seriously. Don't become the problem. Think outside the box and find new solutions to life's encounters.

"There are three ways to ultimate success:
    The first way is to be kind.
    The second way is to be kind.
    The third way is to be kind." Mr. Rogers

With Music, All Things Are Possible

Music is mystical.

It stimulates the mind. It calms and relaxes the soul.

Music allows us to feel all the emotions we experience within our hearts. Furthermore, it can help us reach the deepest turbulences in our thoughts.

Music especially matters to teenagers. It has a significant influence on their behavior, their beliefs, and their bonding. It intensifies and alters their moods, dominates their conversations, and provides entertainment at their social gatherings.

Studies reveal that teenagers listen to music or watch music videos from two to five hours a day. So, how do we connect with the 'plugged-in' and 'tuned-out' teenagers without sounding judgmental about the music they 'love'?

We can start by showing a genuine interest. Ask:

"What is your favorite song?

"Who is your favorite singer?

"Why?"

Wait for the answers. Pay attention. Consider their choices, their role models, and their mood seekers. Try not to be judgmental. Listen and learn.

We can add the magic of laughter by first sharing some of the funny songs we remember. The more serious songs we listened to that our parents disagreed with can come later. Let's just concentrate on the music that helps people have fun and feel good.

Perhaps we can begin with *Gitarzan* written and sung by Ray Stevens in 1969. The funny entertaining music video is on YouTube. It was one of his greatest hits. Two of the song's ten lyrics are:

He's free as the breeze

He's always at ease

He lives in the jungle and hangs by his knees

As he swings through the trees
With a trapeze in his B.V.D.s
Gitarzan, he's a guitar man
He's all you can stand
Give him a hand, Gitarzan

Comments about Ray below the video on YouTube were:
"I like how Ray did the girl singing, the howl for Tarzan, the gorilla and everything."
"This guy was cool before cool became cool. He wrote great cool songs."

Ray's songs *Ahab the Arab, The Streak, The Mississippi Squirrel Revival* and *Everything is Beautiful* round out the top five of his greatest hits. Two beautiful stanzas of *Everything is Beautiful* are:
Everything is beautiful in its own way
Like a starry summer night
or a snow covered winter's day
Everybody's beautiful in their own way
Under God's heaven,
the world's gonna find a way
There is none so blind
as those who will not see
We must not close our minds,
we must let our thoughts be free
For every hour that passes by,
you know the world gets a little older
It's time to realize that beauty lies
in the eyes of the beholder
Two comments about this music video on YouTube were:
"This song makes me wanna get along with someone."

"Did you know when this song came out in the 1970s, most radio stations wouldn't play it? Not because it was bad or anything like that, but because the song didn't fit Ray Stevens' genre of goof-ball tunes. They figured it wouldn't have a chance. But as you know, it ended up becoming the best-recognized and enduring song of his quite long career."

Have fun with the novelty song *Beep, Beep, the Nash Rambler* first sung by The Playmates in 1958. The song begins s-l-o-w-l-y:

While riding in my Cadillac, what to my surprise,
 A little Nash Rambler was following me,
 about one-third my size.
The guy must have wanted it to pass me up
As he kept on tooting his horn. Beep! Beep!
I'll show him that a Cadillac is not a car to scorn.
Refrain:
Beep. Beep. (Beep, Beep.)
Beep, Beep. (Beep, Beep.)
His horn went, beep, beep, beep. (Beep! Beep!)

Three more verses and refrains follow as the music beat goes faster and faster and faster, and the Rambler chases the Cadillac, until the final verse:

Now we're doing a hundred and twenty, as fast as I could go.

The Rambler pulled alongside of me as if I were going slow.

The fellow rolled down his window and yelled for me to hear,

Hey, buddy, how can I get this car out of second gear?

The song was written be Carl Cicchetti and Donald Claps. Kids everywhere love to move around the room s-l-o-w-l-y at first and then faster and faster as the song speeds up to a ridiculously fast speed. Find it on

YouTube. Exercise with it. Get everyone moving. Have fun.

Then there's the *Hokey Pokey*. Everyone enjoyed moving to that song ---- except Milo. He hung his head and said, "I used to be addicted to the Hokey Pokey --- then I turned myself around."

The *Purple People Eater* is a song written be Sheh Wooley in 1958. It's another funny song to share. Sheh wrote this song in a matter of minutes after a child shared an outer space purple eater joke he had heard at school. It goes like this:

Well, I saw the thing comin' out of the sky
It had the one long horn, one big eye
I commenced to shakin' and I said "ooh-see"
It looks like a purple eater to me
It was a one-eyed, one-horned,
flyin' purple people eater
(One-eyed, one-horned,
flyin' purple people eater)
A one-eyed, one-horned,
flyin' purple people eater
Sure looks strange to me (one eye?)
When he came down to earth and he lit in a tree
I said Mr. Purple People Eater, don't eat me
I heard him say in a voice so gruff
"I wouldn't eat you 'cause you're so tough"

The song continues through five more stanzas until the last one which says:

Well, he went on his way, and then what do ya know?
I saw him last night on a TV show
He was blowing it out, really knockin' em dead
Playin' rock and roll music
through the horn in his head

"Tequila!"

Listen to it on YouTube. Music lovers of all ages will like the beat and laugh at the silly song. Comments on YouTube were:

"I was obsessed with this as a kid so I'm here for nostalgia."

"I'm a two-eyed, no-horned regular glazed doughnut eater."

"I used to sing this to my sister saying she was a one-eyed, one-horned --- she would get so-o-o-o mad. Ha Ha."

Kids' song writer Bryant Oden wrote funny songs for kids of all ages. *Paula, the Koala* is one of Bryant Oden's happy song. Another happy song he wrote is *I Got a Pea*. It goes like this:

Today for show and tell
I'm so excited I might yell.
Can't wait to show you it's so cool.
I went to grandmas yesterday,
worked in her garden the whole day,
she let me
Bring some veggies here to school.
I got a carrot, I got a yam.
I got a green bean, fresh not from a can.
Got a potato and as you can probably see;
I also got a pea,
I got a pea,
Why is everyone laughing at me?
So if you find a little pea
on the floor after I leave,
I think it probably belongs to me.
I got a pumpkin, I got a squash
I got some lettuce, I still need to wash
I got an onion and some broccoli;
I also got a pea.

I got a pea.
I got a pea.
Why is everyone laughing at me?
So if you find a little pea
on the floor after I leave,
I think it probably belongs to me.
Yes if you find a little pea
on the floor after I leave,
I think it probably belongs to me.

Two windmills were standing in a field. One asked
the other, "What kind of music do you like?"
The other one said, "I'm a big heavy metal fan."

Ricardo recently said. "I used to be in a band called
"Sold Out". Our gig posters looked great, but no one
ever came."

And Luke said, "Me and my friends have just
formed a band. We call ourselves "999 Megabytes".
We haven't got a gig yet!"

How do you make a bandstand?
Take away their chairs.

Why couldn't Betty open her piano?
All of the keys were locked inside.

Stay involved in what teenagers are listening to.
Share a variety of music. Listen together.
Try to influence teenagers, not control them.
Influence operates internally. Control is imposed from
the outside.

Creating their own music is valuable learning. Set them down at a keyboard or piano and teach them how to play their own songs.

Each of our three children started taking piano lessons when they started attending school. Every evening after school, they were required to practice thirty minutes on their music assignment. They did not have to practice on Saturday or Sunday. We set the timer on the kitchen oven and it buzzed at the end of thirty minutes. It was a learning session as well as a self-discipline session, a reminder to do what you were assigned to do.

Our younger son was practicing one evening after school when the buzzer sounded to end his thirty minutes session, and I heard him say in a happy voice, "The sweetest sound I ever heard!"

The kids were introduced to the many types of music from hip-hop to country, folk to contemporary, inspirational to classical and so much more. If they had not learned a little bit about classical music, they would not have understood these jokes.

"What do you get if Bach dies and is reincarnated as twins?"

"A pair of Re-Bachs."

"Why don't you know where Mozart is buried?"
"Because he's Haydn."

"Why did Mozart get rid of his chickens?"
"Because they ran around screeching, "Bach! Bach! Bach!"

A chicken walked into a library, stopped at the desk and said, "Buk."

So the librarian gave him a book.

This went on nine more times.

Finally the librarian took a break. She stepped outside in back where there was a pond and was shocked at what she saw.

The chicken stood on the edge of the pond, tossing the books to a frog sitting on a lily pad in the pond and squawking, "Buk. Buk."

And the frog threw each and every book into the pond as he said, "Reddit. Reddit."

What do you call a chicken staring at a salad?
Chicken sees-a- salad.

No more chicken jokes. I promise!

Harmony in music and harmony in the family make for a happy life. How to achieve harmony takes lots of practice and oodles of patience.

Homework in our household was not always harmonious. When I was a teenager, I lived by the inner rule "Get the worse done first, then you can play". Therefore doing my homework first was my priority. (It also got me out of doing the dishes after dinner.)

Then we had teenagers and I learned the real meaning of the word 'procrastination'.

After dinner, I would say to my son, "do you have your homework done?' And he would reply, "No. I'll do it later."

I gave him an article to read on how to overcome procrastination. A few days later I asked him, "Have you read the article?"

"No," he said. "I'll do it later."

I turned to my husband and said, "I can't believe that our son doesn't do his homework."

My husband looked at me and smiled. "I can," he said.

To one of my children, "I said, "Are you EVER going to get your homework done?"

And he said, "Relax."

Relax? He wanted me to relax? That was the most unrelaxing word I ever heard. I wanted to yell at him. I wanted to 'ground' him for life. Then I thought of harmony, and the words kindness and respect. So, in a kind voice I respectfully said, "No car until you turn in your homework and bring that grade up. I'll be taking you to school."

He understood the rules. Having a car to drive was a privilege not a birthright.

One week later, all his homework was up to date, his grades were much improved, and he was driving himself to school. We were living in harmony.

Excuses abound for students not getting their homework done and handed in to the teacher. The following are just a few.

"My dog ate it."

"My cat and dog both ate it."

"I thought I'd do my homework tomorrow because I'll be older and wiser."

"I had a cold over the weekend and I was sneezing a lot. I didn't want you to get sick if I sneezed on my homework before I turned it in, so I didn't do it."

"My homework slipped out of my hands and blew away. That's also why I'm late for school. I was chasing my homework."

"I left my homework in the back of my truck when I went through the car wash. The water washed it all away."

"I asked my teacher if I would be scolded for something I didn't do," Sam said. "She said 'no'. So I told her I didn't do my homework."

"I accidently ripped up my homework assignment about the history of perforated paper. It was 'tearable'."

"I heard you say do your homework and I did it. But I didn't hear you say hand it in. So I left it at home."

I tried helping our teenagers with their homework to make our family life more harmonious when they were studying the metric system. "Mom, did you know that the U.S. is one of only three countries out of the 207 countries on earth that does not use the metric system?"

"No, I didn't," I replied.

"Do you know the other two countries?"

"Now, if I didn't know the answer to your first question, why would you expect me to know the other two countries?" I asked.

"Right," the youngest one said. "The other countries are Myanmar and Liberia".

Then they decided to teach me simple metric. One asked, "Mom, if it's thirty degrees Celsius outside, do you wear a bikini or a parka?"

I replied, "I don't wear a bikini no matter what it is outside."

"Don't be funny, Mom. We're serious. You need to learn how to convert. If Celsius is 30 degrees, we multiply that by nine-fifths and add 32 to get the outside temperature of 86 degrees Fahrenheit. Understand?"

At that point, I walked away, but they followed me. "Mom, here's an easy one. My temperature is 37 degrees Celsius. Do I have a fever?"

"I don't know," I said. "Let me feel your forehead."

They gave up teaching me Celsius and turned to the meter length. "A good woman's figure measurement in metric would be 91, 60, 91 centimeters."

"Sounds overweight to me," I said.

"It's easy. You just multiply inches by 2.54. Let's see, Mom. You're measurements would be 89, 68.5, 100 and ---"

"Never mind," I interrupted. "Now I KNOW I don't like metrics."

"Wait, Mom. How many kilometers will your car travel on 20 liters of gasoline?" asked another smarty.

"How should I know?" I all but shouted.

"Convert, Mom, convert," said another.

"I don't want to," I said.

"You should. How will you know when your car needs more gas if the U.S. converts to the metric system?"

"The same way I know now. When one of you teenager drivers lets me finally have the car because the gauge says empty, and the car coughs and dies on the way to the gas station."

"Hold everything. You'll like kilograms, Mom."

"I doubt it."

"When we know the pounds, we multiply by 45/100. You would weigh only 58.5 kilograms."

"Hmmm," I said. "That does sounds better. Maybe the metric system isn't so bad after all."

My friend Grace said to her teenage daughter, "After you finish your homework, we need to talk about something I saw on your IPhone."

It's been three days and her daughter is still doing her homework.

Ethan was doing geometry homework with music coming from his Bluetooth speaker volume turned to full blast when his father walked in the front door. "Hey, Dad," he shouted. "Listen to that. Did you ever in your life hear anything to compare to that?"

"Only once," his dad shouted back. "When I was a boy a truck loaded with metal trash cans hit another truck loaded with pigs, ducks and dogs. It sounded just like that noise coming from your Bluetooth speaker.

You may question the iffy lyrics of some of the music your teenagers are listening to, but there's not a lot you can do about it.

Stay involved in what they are listening to. Remind them that the rude, trashy words they may hear will forever become a part of their thoughts, thoughts they should strive to not dwell on or repeat. People with Alzheimer's disease may forget everything else, but they will still remember the music.

Share their music.

Share your music.

Listen together.

The basic rules for listening are: display mutual respect. Expect to be tested. Negotiate and agree on rules in advance. Be kind.

"All music is folk music. I never did hear a horse sing a song."
     Louis Armstrong, famous Musician

"I know only two tunes: one of them is 'Yankee Doodle', and the other isn't."
     President U. S. Grant

Billie went to see an Elvis impersonator, but he got there too late --- he had already left the building.

Josh Groban singing 'You Raise Me Up' is a beautiful song to listen to. The lyrics were written in 2002 by Brenda Graham, an Irish song writer. The first two stanzas are:
    When I was down, and, oh, my soul, so weary
    When troubles come, and my heart burdened be
    Then, I am still and wait here in the silence
    Until you come and sit awhile with me

You raise me up, so I can stand on mountains
You raise me up to walk on stormy seas
I am strong when I am on your shoulders
You raise me up to more than I can be

Comments about this song on YouTube were:
"This song always makes me cry."
"This song makes me want to believe in God again."
"It hurts when the person who gave you your best memories becomes only a memory."
"If you don't play this at my funeral, I'm not going."
"I played this at my hamster's funeral."
An all-time favorite song is *Let There Be Peace on Earth* written by Jill Jackson-Miller and Sly Miller in 1955. It was initially written for and sung by the International Children's Choir.

The song is performed worldwide all year long, but many still consider it a Christmas song. Country music singer Vince Gill and his daughter Jenny first sang the song in 1993. He dedicated the song and the album of the same name to his brother who had just died after suffering for years from injuries received in an auto accident. A few of the lyrics are:

Let there be peace on earth
And let it begin with me
Let there be peace on earth
The peace that was meant to be
With God as our Father
Brothers all are we
Let me walk with my brother
In perfect harmony.
Let peace begin with me
Let this be the moment now.
With every step I take
Let this be my solemn vow

To take each moment and live
Each moment in peace eternally
Let there be peace on earth
And let it begin with me.

Peace begins with a smile.   Mother Teresa

The Family That Travels Together, Unravels Together

"How many more miles?"

"Are we there yet?"

"How much longer?

When I heard those questions from one teenager or another, I knew we were in the car, or van, or motorhome and on our way. The family vacation had begun. And the family that travels together, unravels together happily so long as laughter, kindness, respect and love are thrown into the travel plans.

At no other time during the year did family members see each other day and night, in such close quarters, with no one else to turn to for entertainment, idle conversation, or companionship. Neither the children nor the parents could talk to someone on the phone without everyone listening in, or could invite friends to stop by for a visit.

With such close togetherness, sibling space issues were bound to happen.

"Mom, he's looking at me again."

"Don't look at your sister."

"Mom, she's touching me."

"Don't touch your brother.

"Mom, it's my turn to sit in the front seat."

"Not yet, son. I'm timing the turns.

The rumbling unrest was almost always the same at the end of a long day traveling together, and the words could become very trying on parental patience. Traveling in such close quarters, we all had to be kind to one another and settle our disputes sensibly because there was no place to get away from each other, on our 'get away' vacation.

Near the end of one long day of traveling, our teenagers started arguing again about who was sitting in whose space.

"That's it!" Their father said. "No more talking. No more sounds. The first one to make a sound has to order last at dinner tonight."

There was a long silence. Then I began to hear movement in the back seat, and turned around. All shapes of facial expressions and types of body movements were being tried to make someone break the imposed silence and become the last to order dinner.

I had to laugh at their antics. They were hilarious.

And that night, I had to wait until last to order dinner. I was the first one to break the silence. Our family's harmony was restored by the laughter and joy we shared.

'Always be joyful.' (1 Thessalonians 5:16 NLT)

The next day, our teenage daughter said, "Dad, let me drive for a while."

"No way, daughter. I want to arrive safely --- wherever we're going."

'Wherever we're going' presented a problem from time to time when we were equipped with map readers (who might mislead us) instead of GPS instructions (which might also mislead us).

My husband hated to admit it when we were lost. He would rather drive aimlessly for hours than stop and ask directions. One summer day, he drove our three teenagers and me into Boston to visit the Common and walk the Freedom Trail. The sites were clearly marked in red on our map of the city, but we could not find them. So, we drove around Boston for hours, and hopelessly tried to find the way.

I asked my husband to stop and get directions, but he wouldn't do it. "I'm not lost," he said. "It has to be here somewhere."

We begged. We pleaded. But he wouldn't stop. Then after we had wasted several hours driving around in circles, he finally pulled over to ask a man on the street.

"Take John R. 'Sterile" Drive," the nice man said with a Boston accent. "You 'caun't' miss it."

He was wrong. We could miss it; and we did. We couldn't even find Sterile Drive on our map, or on any of the many street signs we passed --- again and again.

Suddenly our older son said, "There it is. We found Boston Common." And he was right. But to this day, we don't know how we got there.

Then we noticed the name of the street we were on. It was John R. <u>Storrow</u> Drive. And we all laughed at our silly confusion. The nice man's Boston accent was foreign to our Midwestern ears. John's Drive was "Storrow" not "Sterile". What a relief.

Later in the day, we tried to go to Lexington and Concord, but we couldn't find our way out of Boston. There were no signs directing tourists to historical sights. Dear old Dad drove us around the city for what seemed like hours. We passed the same buildings again and again, but he refused to stop and ask for directions. We pleaded with him. And we begged. Finally, he gave in and stopped at the next service station.

He soon came out with a puzzled look on his face. "I'll have to go somewhere else," he said. "I couldn't understand their Boston accent."

At the second station, he came out shaking his head. "Same thing," he said.
"I couldn't understand them."

At the third station, he said, "Give me a pencil and paper. I'm getting this in writing." It worked. He understood their writing. We found Lexington and Concord before dark. Then, after exploring the historical sites Mom and Dad chose to visit, it was our teenagers' turn to decide what to do. They all agreed on the latest Indiana Jones movie.

"We'll have to ask someone how to get there," I said.

"Not me!" My husband said, shaking his head.

So I had to do it. At the next service station, I went inside. The attendant was very helpful. I listened to every word he said, then returned to the van. "I understood his words," I said. "But I don't know what they mean."

"Tell us," shouted the kids. "We'll figure it out."

"Okay. We're to go back the way we came and pass the Ho Jo ---."

"The Howard Johnson where we're staying ---," they said.

"Then we go onto the rotary ---."

"Oh, no," moaned Driver Dad. "Not another rotary. If we get on the inside lane, we'll be circling all night long."

I ignored his moans. "--- and take the second left. The theater is about a mile down the road, over two dips and on the right."

"Got it," said the kids. "Start driving, Dad. We'll get you there. And you won't even have to ask for directions again."

They did it, just in time for the 7:00 feature.

But being lost in Boston left its mark. My husband was worse than ever before. He NEVER wanted to ask for directions again. No matter how much we pleaded with him, or begged him to stop, he just kept on driving, and, with a smile on his face, said, "I'm not asking for directions and I'm not lost because wherever you go, there you are."

We shared the laughter. Sharing the laughter is half the fun. In fact, most laughter doesn't come from just hearing jokes, but rather from spending time with family and friends. We can't share a laugh with others unless we are really involved with them.

When we care enough to really connect face to face, we're engaging in a process that puts the brakes on defensive anger, resentment and stress. And if we look for the laughter to share as well, we'll all feel happier and more relaxed, even on the family vacation where we are temporarily unable to alter the stressful situation. Laughing together adds joy to any new and exciting family experience. Try taking along a 'trips jar' filled with travel-related jokes, then when the going gets tough, as it sometimes will, ask one of the teenagers to pull out a joke and read it, sharing the laughter with everyone. Let's start with these few examples to share:

Misty asked Julian, "Where did your mom go on vacation?"

"Alaska," said Julian.

"Oh, never mind," said Misty in a huff. "I'll ask her myself."

A book never written was titled *Where to Stay on Vacation* by Moe Tell

A book never written was titled *Vacations Are So Expensive* by Seymour Foreless

A book never written was titled *Yellow River* by I. P. Freely.

A book never written was titled *Beneath the Bleachers* by Seymour Butts

Jimmy asked Joey, "Why can't basketball players go on vacation?"

"I don't know," said Joey. "Why?"

"They always get called for traveling!"

"My son came to visit for summer vacation," said Violet.

"How nice," replied Sue. "Did you meet him at the airport?"

"Of course not, Silly Sue. I've known him all his life!"

A young man on vacation in the mountains decided to go horseback riding. He visited a local rancher who rented out horses to ride in the mountains. The rancher was a very religious man. He explained to the visitor that in order to make the horse go, he'd have to say "Thank God", and to make the horse stop, he should shout, "Amen."

During his ride, the horse was stung by a wasp. In fear and pain, the horse took off running right toward a dangerous cliff.

"Amen!" shouted the man, hanging onto the horse for dear life.

The horse stopped just a few inches away from the edge of the cliff. The young man caught his breath, looked over the cliff, and muttered out loud, "Thank God."

A woman was on vacation with her mother. She called her husband back home and asked, "How's everything?"

Her husband said, "It's bad. First of all, your cat died."

The woman was upset. "You could have broken the news to me when I got home," she cried. "Now I can't enjoy my vacation. You could have just told a little lie, like the cat's on the roof and you can't get her down."

"Okay, I'm sorry," said her husband. "I'll remember that."

Then the woman said, "How's Dad doing?"

And the husband replied, "Your Dad's on the roof and we can't get him down."

A tourist was being led through the swamps of Florida. "Is it true," he asked, "that an alligator won't attack you if you are carrying a flashlight?"

"That depends on how fast you're carrying the flashlight," replied the guide.

A woman interrupted their vacation to go to the dentist. "I want a tooth pulled, and I don't want Novocain because I'm in a hurry," she said. "Just pull the tooth as fast as possible so we can go on our way."

"You certainly are a brave woman," the surprised dentist said. "Which tooth is it?"

The woman turned to her husband and said, "Show him the tooth, Dear."

Frank was in charge of ringing the bell in the bell tower. He wanted to go on vacation but he had to find someone to ring the bell for him each day, or he couldn't go. After looking for several days, he hadn't found anyone willing to do it.

He finally gave up and went to his computer to cancel his vacations plans. Suddenly there was a knock on his door. When he answered, he found an armless man standing on the porch. "Can I help you? " He asked.

"I'm here for the bell tower job, please."

"I'm sorry I have to ask this," Frank said, "but how are you going to ring the bell?"

"I can do it. I know I can. Come to the tower and I'll show you," said the armless man.

"Well, okay," said Frank in a cautious voice.

They went to the tower and climbed to the top.

The armless man ran as fast as he could toward the bell. He jumped up and hit the bell with his face. It rang loud and clear, as if someone with arms had rung it.

"My goodness, if that doesn't hurt, you can have the job. Thank you."

Frank enjoyed a week on an island. He arrived home late at night on the day before he was scheduled to go back to ringing the bell. Early the next morning, two police officers were standing at his door.

"Can I help you, officers?" He asked.

"A man was found dead on the ground beneath the bell tower," one of the officers said. "It looks like he fell from the top. Can you identify the body?"

Frank rode with the policemen to the bell tower. He got out of the car and walked over to the body.

"Do you know this man?" Asked one of the officers.

"I don't know him," said Frank. "But his face rings a bell."

Two tourists were driving through Louisiana. As they were approaching Natchitoches they started arguing about the pronunciation of the town. They argued back and forth until they stopped for lunch. As they stood at the counter one tourist asked the employee, "Before we order, could you please settle an argument for us? Would you please pronounce where we are --- very slowly?"

The girl leaned over the counter and said, "Daairrrryyy Quueeeeennn"

The teacher called on Devon during class. "Would you please use the words letter carrier in a sentence?"

"Yes, Ma'am," Devon said. "My Dad said that after seeing how many things my Mom was bringing on vacation, he would rather letter carrier own luggage."

A group of hikers were being led through the wilderness by a guide. On the fifth day, the hikers noticed that they were going around in circles.

"Hey, we're lost!" One of the hikers shouted. "You said you were the best guide in the United States."

"I am," the guide replied. "But I think we may have wandered into Canada."

We usually planned for our next summer vacation sometime in January, during a snowstorm, when everyone in the family had to stay home and no unexpected visitors would be dropping by. Our family meeting was held around the kitchen table.

The question was: "where will we go on our vacation this summer?"

The ideas poured in: Virgin Islands, Europe, Hawaii, South America, or Alaska. Then we got realistic. Where could we afford to go on our vacation this summer? That narrowed the choices considerably.

Planning was a big part of our vacation fun. By starting in January, we could decide to coordinate visits to historical sites, zoos, amusement parks, golf courses, museums, zoos, amusement parks, and golf courses. It was difficult as you can tell, but we tried to stay with the 'educational first, fun later' plan. Then, when decisions were agreed upon by everyone, we had six months of anticipation, reading brochures, studying travel guides, and making advance reservations.

On one family trip, we didn't make motel reservations for the first night out on a 12 day road trip through the New England states. We had reservations for the second night on 42nd street in Manhattan, New York. But, for the first night, we had decided to drive for about 400 miles, then find a place to stay somewhere in Ohio along Interstate 70.

That was our first mistake.

We loaded the family van and left on schedule. With a horseshoe-shaped sofa in the back, a small sink and refrigerator along one side, and four captain chairs toward the front, there was lots of room for all of us to ride in comfort. It was raining as we drove through Indiana and Ohio. But the rain didn't dampen our happy holiday spirits. We arrived at Columbus, Ohio before dark and decided to drive on for another hour before finding a motel.

That was our second mistake.

It started to rain harder. Then we were in a terrible downpour. We couldn't see the road in front of us. "I'm getting a room at the next town we come to," announced Dad, the driver.

At the next town, we found a motel and Dad went inside. He soon came out and ran to the van in the rain. "All of the motels are full for miles around," he said. "We're in the middle of a flash flood."

"Let's go on," I said optimistically. "We'll surely find a place as soon as we drive out of this rain."

But we didn't drive out of the rain. It went on for miles and miles.

It grew dark, and the storm grew worse. Electrical lines were blown down. The power was out in every city we passed. We couldn't find any motels in the dark, and there were no bright lights on billboards to show us the way. We had to keep going on, into the stormy night.

The rain finally stopped near Wheeling, West Virginia and we pulled into a motel. But it was full. All of the rooms in town were taken. Travelers had stopped early for the night when they heard of the flash floods in Ohio.

We drove on to Washington, Pennsylvania. It was almost midnight. My husband had driven nearly 600 miles in pounding rain. He was exhausted. He stopped the van at a motel, and went inside for reservations.

Soon, he came out shaking his head. "No room," he said. "Box-car Willie's in town."

"Who's Box-car Willie?" We asked in unison.

"Some country western singer that everybody in Pennsylvania really likes – but I don't like him very much right now."

"What are we going to do? "Asked our daughter.

"Make the best of things," I said. "The motel has a lighted parking lot. Let's sleep in the van for a few hours then drive on to New York City.

One slept on the floor, two in the horseshoe sofa, and two in reclining captain's chairs in front. It was a warm night and we had to sleep in our clothes, but no one complained. We did what we had to do.

At 5:00 a.m., our youngest teenager woke up with a start. "Dad, I need a bathroom," he said. "Now!"

Dad drove to the front door of an all-night restaurant, and we all filed into their bathrooms, looking as if we had slept in the van --- which, of course, we had.

We then traveled on to New York City and arrived at our reserved room at one in the afternoon. Luck was with us. The room was ready, and we lined up at the bathroom door to wait for our turn in the shower before going out to see the Empire State Building and Macy's enormous Department Store.

Memories were made of this. I remember another rainy Saturday night on another vacation when we stayed in the sleaziest motel in Huntington, West Virginia. We were traveling in a car. We had not made advance reservations, and again due to torrential rains, it was the only place left in town.

We had two bedrooms and two bathrooms, but the plumbing didn't work in one bathroom, and the plaster was falling off the ceiling in the other one. The beds were clean, but the floors and walls were not. By the light of a bare bulb hanging from the bathroom ceiling, my husband took one look at the working sink and said, "It's filthy. I'm not shaving here in the morning."

When I opened a window for some fresh air, the smell from a rotting garbage heap out back nearly gagged us. Just as I was turning out the light for the night, I saw our younger son chewing on the faded blue spread on the bed. "Get that out of your mouth," I said. "Do you want to catch some terrible disease?"

In the dark of the night, we were all awakened by an ambulance siren screaming by our door. My husband jumped up and looked out.

From the bed in the other room, our older son said, "Did the ambulance stop here?"

"No," said his dad. "It went on by."

"Good," he said, with a sigh of relief. "I thought someone in the motel had caught that terrible disease Mom warned us about."

My husband started putting on his shoes.

"What are you doing?" I asked.

"I'm getting out of here while I still can," he said

"But it's 2:00 in the morning. The kids are going back to sleep."

"Wake them. We all slept in our clothes. We're getting out of here NOW. They can sleep in the car."

Ten minutes later, we were in the car and happily heading for home, grateful that we had survived our short Saturday night stay at the sleaziest motel in town.

When our family was traveling before GPS equipped abilities, I was the official reader of the maps. My husband had always said that I was an 'expert' at telling him where to go. And I did have my moments. Some of those were good. Others were bad. Naturally, it was the bad ones my family remembered.

I used to take great pride in the fact that I always had a sense of direction. I knew what direction we were going without even consulting a compass. Then one day we traveled into Indianapolis on our way home from a vacation in Northern Michigan. I was driving at the time, and my husband was reading the map. The streets were crowded with rush hour traffic. We stopped at an intersection. "Do I turn left here for Illinois?" I asked.

"Not according to the map," he said, studying it in front of him. "Illinois is right."

"You must have the map upside down," I said. "I'm turning left. My sense of direction is never wrong."

He threw the map on the floor. "Okay. Fine! Don't listen to me. Just go ahead and do it your way," he said, and stared straight ahead.

I turned left and, for miles, we crept along in heavy traffic. Finally, at the edge of the city, I saw a sign that read: Columbus, Ohio – 170 miles. "Oh, no," I said. "We're going the wrong way."

My husband didn't say a word.

As I pulled into a nearby service station to turn around, I said, "I hate this traffic. Will you drive now?"

He shook his head and said, "Not until you get us back to where you turned the wrong way".

I did. And he took over from there. Then I apologized profusely for not trusting his map reading abilities.

My confidence was shattered that day, and my family didn't forget it. They enjoyed teasing me about the mistake I made on the <u>very last day</u> that I thought my sense of direction was never wrong.

Our family enjoyed the game of teasing one another. But everyone who wanted to participate in the game had to remember to follow this one rule very carefully. <u>Don't dish it out, if you can't take it</u>. In other words, if you want to tease, you must be able to take the teasing.

And, because I liked to tease others, I had to take it, with laughter, when my family teased me about the 'memorable moments' I had given them in the past.

"Remember when we were in the Black Hills and Mom said, "Look kids. There's <u>R</u>ount <u>M</u>ushmore. She was so funny!"

And everyone laughed, even though they have remembered *that* moment a thousand times before.

"Remember the time in the desert when Mom thought the humidity gauge in our motorhome was stuck on zero, and she hurt her hand pounding on it, until we convinced her that there was no humidity in the hot, dry desert."

Very Funny!

"How about the time Mom was carrying little brother's large bull horns out of Mexico, across the Rio Grande River bridge, and gored a border policeman in the crowd? Wasn't that funny when he wouldn't believe it was an accident?"

Give it a rest, boys. Give it a rest. Funny is, as funny does.

The boys had a lot of fun teasing their older sister about everything. One subject of their teasing was cemeteries. Yes, cemeteries.

When we were riding along a highway in Mississippi, she admired three tall crosses set high on a hill in a huge cemetery along the side of the road. After that day, whenever her brothers saw a field of tombstones, they would turn to her and say, "Oh look, Sis. A cemetery! Your favorite thing."

Her brothers have pointed out many cemeteries to her during our journeys, probably too many. And yet, if the boys happened to miss one along the way, her dad and I found ourselves joining in the teasing fun, pointing out cemeteries as we rode along.

When the children were younger, we took three trips in a 28-foot motorhome fully equipped with a big refrigerator full of food for the hungry, running water from a faucet for the thirsty, and a handy bathroom for those who couldn't wait.

When we stopped for the night, fellow campers were extremely friendly. A one-night neighbor boiled two rotten duck eggs for our sons to take home with them. And, for a farewell gift, she gave me a small can of 'razorback sow's milk'. I still have it. Somewhere.

Another neighbor discussed his Jewish beliefs, told us about his motorhome trips throughout the United States and, over an evening card game of Bridge, he invited us to travel through Canada with him, his wife and three young daughters.

But we didn't. It wasn't on our schedule.

When we drove the motorhome down to Laredo, Texas, we parked it in three parking spaces, and walked across the border into Nuevo Laredo to begin our first visit to Mexico. My husband didn't enjoy bargaining over the prices there. But I did. A peddler stopped me on the street and offered to sell the kids a woven vest for five dollars each. I shook my head and said, "It's too hot to wear vests today," and I turned to walk away.

"One moment," he said. "For you, four dollars each."

I shook my head 'no'.

"Three dollars and that's as low as I can go," he said.

I wouldn't give over three dollars for all three," I replied.

"Sold!" shouted the man. He gave me the vests and held out his hand for the money.

He was happy. So was I. But who out-bargained whom? I didn't want to buy those vests in the first place.

We traveled from Laredo, to Houston and the Astrodome, then on to Galveston Beach and the Gulf of Mexico. To get to New Orleans from there after riding the ferry across water, I mapped out our way along what looked to be a scenic, relaxing road on the Gulf shores.

The road was definitely scenic, and narrow, not at all relaxing for my husband who was driving a long and wide motorhome. There wasn't much traffic. Thank God for that. The road was too narrow for two vehicles to meet. My husband had to stop the motorhome along the side of the road when we met another car, or when we had to let someone behind us pass.

He mumbled a lot under his breath, and seemed to be more than a little upset with me. But how was I to know? On the map, the road looked like a graceful black line along the beautiful Gulf of Mexico.

For our second trip in the motorhome, we went out west through the Teton Mountains, Yellowstone Park, and Black Hills.

The third trip was in California, enjoying Disneyland, Universal Studios, Fisherman's Wharf, and more. In San Francisco, I wanted to see Chinatown before we crossed the Golden Gate Bridge on our way to the Redwood Forest. My husband was driving, and I was reading the map, but we couldn't find Chinatown. "According to the map, we should be there," I said. "But I don't see it. Do you?"

My husband shook his head.

"There's a tunnel," I said, pointing to the right. "Take it. Maybe Chinatown is somewhere on the other side."

He drove the huge motorhome through a long dark tunnel and came out on the other side --- right in the middle of Chinatown. The streets were VERY narrow, and crowded bumper-to-bumper with cars. A truck was parked in the street, delivering fresh fish. It held up traffic for 20 minutes.

"Chinatown is no place for a big motorhome," moaned my husband. "Get me out of here."

Studying the map, I said, "Take the next right. That should get us back to a main highway."

At the next right, I heard my husband groan. I glanced up. Ahead of us was a steep San Francisco street going straight up toward the sky. He accused me of deliberately choosing the steep street for more of my 'authentic atmosphere'. But how was I to know? The map showed it as a straight black line with no ups and downs.

"I hope we make it," he said, shifting the motorhome into a low, low gear.

We inched up the hill with traffic beside us, in front of us, and behind us. At the top, we came to a stop sign. Dad, the driver, stopped the motorhome on the steep street behind the stop sign line, as any law-abiding citizen should do.

"I hope the brakes hold," he said through clenched teeth. "There's a little yellow car right behind us. I hope I don't roll backwards over it when I try to take off."

I watched out the back window as he gave the motor full power for take-off. We edged safely forward and didn't crush the little yellow car behind us.

Later, we learned that drivers, who are accustomed to the steep streets in San Francisco, try to stop their vehicles on level ground in the intersections, beyond the stop sign lines, if they are the first ones in line. But we didn't know that. We were tourists, doing as tourists often do, on their first trip to the steep city.

So, how did we survive our family vacations, when we put all the kids in the car, left our comfortable house (with a bedroom for each teenager and three separate bathrooms), and paid by the night to stay cooped up together in a motorhome or a tiny motel room, with just one bathroom for five people?

We stayed kind, and considerate, and tried not to lose our sense of humor.

Traveling with teenagers on a family vacation offered a great opportunity to spend time together, and to interact with one another in caring, loving ways.

Games, 'trip jar' jokes, and music made it fun. We often played the music *Baby Elephant Walk* and *The Pink Panther Theme*, both by Henry Mancini. The music was lively and happy, the notes harmonious. We all enjoyed listening to it as we traveled to new horizons, unraveling and laughing together.

'Music is the art of the prophets, the only art that can calm the agitations of the soul; it is one of the most magnificent and delightful presents God has given us.'
Martin Luther

Dates, Heartbreaks, and Fears

Helping our teenagers become independent, caring and happy adults is no small task. Teens start learning from birth how to behave by watching their parents and extended family members. It's important that they learn how to cope with dates, heartbreaks and fears in positive ways to become resilient adults.

As children, we laugh hundreds of times a day, but as adults, life tends to become more serious and laughter less frequent. By seeking out more opportunities to laugh, we can improve our emotional health, strengthen our relationships, find greater happiness, and even add years to our lives.

Laughter is good for our health. It relaxes the whole body. A hearty laugh relieves stress and relaxes our muscles for up to 40 minutes.

Laughter protects the heart by improving the function of blood vessels thus increasing the blood flow which can help prevent a heart attack and other cardiovascular problems.

Laughter helps mend heartbreaks, heartaches, and downheartedness.

Luther was brokenhearted. His girlfriend had left him. She worked in a zoo. He thought she was a keeper.

"I once dated a girl with a lazy eye. Turned out she was seeing someone else on the side."

After my boyfriend and I broke up, I was so sad that I watched my dog chase his tail for 30 minutes and I thought, "Wow, animals are easily entertained."

Then I realized I just watched my dog chase his tail for 30 minutes.

"I don't have a girlfriend. But I do know a girl who will be mad at me for saying that."

"When is it appropriate for a teenager like me to ask, "Where is this relationship going?"

"When he's been captured by pirates and the ship's name is 'Relationship'."

My ex-girlfriend just texted me: Wish you were here.

She does that every time she walks through a cemetery.

Saying "Have a nice day" to someone sounds friendly, but when my ex-boyfriend says, "Enjoy your next twenty-four hours" it sounds threatening.

Be it good or bad, relationship and sex education began at home when the children were very young, long before they grew into those heartfelt teenage years. Even before they learned to talk, children entered the first stage of sexual awareness.

So, when children start asking questions about the facts of life, it is imperative to answer them with openness and honesty.

Words on television heard by young children can pose a problem for concerned parents. "What does raped mean, Mommy? That bruised woman on TV said she was raped."

"Ah-h-h, rape is when a person abuses another person's body without permission."

"You mean like a man pushing you down the stairs when you don't want to go and it hurts you?"

"Yeah, something like that ----------."

"Dad, why did everyone in the police station on TV laugh when the woman said she was a virgin? What's a virgin?" asked one child.

"And why did the policeman call her a whore?" asked another.

"Virgin and whore are opposite," their dad said.

"Opposite? Opposite what?"

"Opposite -------- words, like no and yes. Let's turn to another TV show."

Our son was eight when he heard a man on television refer to the sexual drive. "What's that? He asked his dad.

"Well," said the man I married. "I think it's a street on the other side of town."

Don't wait to tell too little too late. We need to face difficult conversations in difficult times.

Dear old Dad later decided it was time to talk about the facts of life. "Son," he said. "Do you know how babies are made?"

"Sure, Dad. Do you want me to tell you about it?"

They then held an interesting interlude, informing each other on the finer points of life.

Our school classmate Cindy found a deck of cards hidden under her seven year old son's bed. The cards were decorated with pictures of topless girls. She showed them to the lad's dad, and his dad said, "Son, from now on, if you get any topless pictures of girls. Don't try to hide them. Bring them to me right away."

He later told Cindy that he didn't want the secretiveness and he would decide what to do with the pictures. But Cindy was left to wonder, "Is he hoping to see more topless pictures like the ones she found under their son's bed?"

A live presentation of the musical HAIR, including nude bodies on stage in the first act, came to our town. "Can I go see it?" asked our young son after he had carefully read the newspaper reviews.

Not wanting to give his dad a chance to say "only if you take me along', I quickly replied. "You're too young."

Our son was momentarily disappointed. Then he shrugged his shoulders, and said, "They're probably all fat anyway."

When our children grew into adolescents, the questions quit coming as often as before. We knew they had them in their minds, but they had become hesitant about asking them openly. The children in our family had advanced to stage two, the three Ws ----- worrying, wondering, and whispering.

They were worrying about the mysterious facts of life, wondering about the birds and the bees, and probably whispering with their friends to find the answers. But they weren't asking us. Why? How much of life and love did our adolescents understand? When our daughter was nine, I talked with her, explaining in detail what she should expect in the near future as outward signs of her approaching womanhood. "Any questions?" I asked.

"No," she replied.

For the next several months, she avoided any serious discussions with me. With sexual implications so widespread and publicly displayed, I knew she had to have unanswered questions. It was only natural. But she wasn't asking me. Where was she gathering her information? And how accurate was it?

Finally, I decided not to wait any longer. "Let's go to my bedroom and have a girl talk," I said.

An hour flew by as we sat on the bed and discussed love, marriage, sex and babies --- in that order. We turned to an anatomy book and studied detailed drawings of the human body. As our girl talk drew to a close, I said, "Any more questions?"

"I don't think so," she said with a smile.

"Any time you have a question, don't hesitate to ask your dad or me," I said.

"Mom?"

"Yes?"

"Thanks for talking to me. Last week, I told my Sunday School teacher that I couldn't talk to my parents about --- things."

"Oh, Honey," I said. "Nobody loves you or wants to talk to you as much as we do."

"I know that now. My teacher will sure be surprised when I tell her about our talk next Sunday."

What was she going to tell her teacher? I didn't ask. I was afraid to know.

When a ten year old is no longer asking, parents need to go on and supply good answers to their unasked questions about sex. If we don't, our child may be finding the wrong answers in the wrong places. Or they may be sexually harassed and not fully understand that they don't have to put up with it. They don't have to be embarrassed or live in fear.

We need to explain to our adolescents that all kinds of people harass. The most frequent types of harassment among adolescents are sexual words, jesters, remarks, or lurid attempts to joke suggestively. The big question is: What can a young person do about it? Here are some answers to share. First and foremost react wisely.

Never put yourself in danger. If you and the harasser are alone in a dim hall, an isolated classroom, or a dark parking lot, get away as soon as possible.

Most harassers, however, will choose to do their harassing in public places. They are not looking to attack physically and will probably be satisfied to make you uncomfortable. Most harassers rely on your good manners to do nothing, which will let them get away with it. So surprise them, speak up. Say, "Hey, I have feelings. I don't understand why you are talking to me like that."

Some harassing may be rotten ideas on how to get your attention. The harasser incorrectly thinks that even bad attention is better than no attention at all.

Be aware. Be safe. Show no fear. If a person is obscenely staring at you, point at him or her and kindly say, "Please stop staring at me."

The important thing is to not be afraid to speak out in public for others to see and hear. Don't allow any physical touching in inappropriate places on your body. Move quickly away and say, "I'm reporting you." Then do it.

Time races on to stage three, the question of teenage knowledge and values. These are the dating years of discovery and doubt when teenagers have to decide about their own sexual attitudes and moral values. Parents must not be afraid to take a firm stand against the permissiveness of today's society. We can offer good advice without sounding preachy.

We need to share our views with kindness and respect. Discuss rules with a loving heart. Teenagers can only know what is expected of them through parent-child communication that leaves no room for misunderstanding or confusion. Any other way is doubtful.

Each teenager is sure to have his or her own special set of 'value' issues. Our daughter was a shy teenager around boys. She wanted to go to the prom, but no one asked her, and she said she'd rather die than ask an underclassman or someone from out of town to take her to the prom. So we made other plans. Not going to the prom wasn't the end of the world. There were lots of people who didn't go to high school proms, and they survived the disappointment, going on to lead happy, productive lives afterwards.

I drove my daughter and some of her friends to dinner and a movie in the city on the night of her junior prom. They laughed a lot and had a wonderful time --- and the entire evening cost a lot less than a new prom dress.

Of course, a new dress and date to the prom might have been fun for her, but the road to self-pity and bitterness is paved with disappointed might-have-been memories. The road to happiness and freedom is paved with making the best of any situation that comes along.

Through the years, our daughter's dad had teased her, telling her that she should wait until she was eighteen to start dating. And she did. It wasn't intentional. It just happened that way. On her second date, the young man drove up as her dad and I were watering the front lawn. He spoke to us on his way to the front door, and I said, "Hello."

After our daughter had let her date into the house, my husband smiled. "I didn't speak to him," he said in a smug voice.

"That wasn't very nice of you," I said. "What's the matter? Don't you like someone dating your little girl?"

He must have given my question some quick thought because when our daughter and her date came out of the house a few minutes later, he told her to be in by midnight and then discussed the latest baseball scores with her nice young man.

One year later, he congratulated our daughter and the same nice young man on their engagement, then he told her, "Be in by midnight. I need my rest. I have to work for a living." You see, he didn't sleep until his 'little girl' was safely home.

Much later, my daughter said to me, "Mom, why didn't you push me to date at an earlier age, like some of my girlfriends' mothers did?"

"You had to become confident in yourself before you were ready to reach out to the opposite sex to build a positive relationship," I said. "No young girl should be pushed to date until she alone feels the time is right for her. You had to overcome your shyness." "Why didn't you tell me to get over my shyness?"

"You had to do it on your own. And you did. If I had pointed it out to you. It might have stayed with you forever. The best thing I could do for you was to 'accentuate the positive to eliminate the negative'.

Wow, I feel a song coming on.

Ac-Cent-Tchu-Ate the Positive

(written and sung by Johnny Mercer published in 1944)

Gather 'round me everybody
Gather 'round me while I'm preachin
Feel a sermon comin' on me
The topic will be sin and that's what I'm ag'in
If you want to hear my story
Then settle back and just sit tight
While I start reviewin'
The attitude of doin' right
You've got to accentuate the positive
Eliminate the negative
And latch on to the affirmative
Don't mess with Mister In-Between

You've got to spread joy up to the maximum
Bring gloom down to the minimum
Have faith or pandemonium's
Liable to walk upon the scene
To illustrate my remark
Jonah in the whale. Noah in the ark
What did they do just when everything looked so dark?
(Man. They said "We'd better accentuate the positive")
(Eliminate the negative")
("And latch on to the affirmative")
Don't mess with Mister In-Between (No!)
Don't mess with Mister In-Between

There are no steadfast, fool-proof rules for parents to use when trying to educate young people on sexual responsibilities. Every person is uniquely different and has to be dealt with according to his or her individual traits. But some statements seem to fit the problems of every teenager at one time or another. Don't be afraid to use them. If a teenager complains, just tell him or her, "I have to say it. I don't enjoy it any more than you do. But I love you. It's my responsibility."

"I don't care if everybody's doing it that still doesn't make it right."

"Don't bring your date to the house when we're gone. Why put yourself in a possible pressure situation?"

"Don't go to your date's house when his (or her) parents are gone."

"Is the party chaperoned? You aren't going if it isn't."

"Try to be home by midnight, but if you're going to be late, give us a call. That makes you a considerate teenager. And if you aren't home on time, we start worrying. That makes us upset parents. You don't want that.

"Where are you going? When will you be back? Please keep us informed of your plans and we'll keep you informed of ours."

"Do you know anything about her (or him)? Who are the parents? "

Who are the parents? I couldn't believe I asked that. But I did. When I was a teenager many years ago, my parents often said to me, "Who are his parents?"

Then I usually replied in an angry voice, "It doesn't matter who his parents are. That doesn't reflect on him."

Unfortunately, when I became the parent of a dating teenager, I found myself asking the same question. Perhaps the trait is hereditary.

Our son met a girl from out of town while he was cruising around in his car on the usual Saturday night circuit when one was sixteen and had recently passed his driver's license test. "She's real cute, Mom," he said, "and she's nineteen."

"Who are her parents?" I asked in my parental-duty voice.

"I don't know, but she graduated last year and she works at the Subway in Middleton."

She came to town again the next weekend and spent the evening cruising with our son and two of his friends. Later, our son said, "I have her telephone number. I'm going to call her and ask her for a date."

"Do you know anything about her family?"

"She has several brothers and sisters."

My son and I went to the Middleton Mall to find him another pair of those all-occasion tennis shoes. We met a pretty young girl pushing a sweet toddler about in a shopping cart. My son gave her a warm smile. "Go on to the shoe store, Mom," he said. "I'll catch up with you later."

I followed his directions and, when he entered the store a few minutes later, he had an unusual frown on his face.

"Who was the girl?" I asked, politely doing my parental-duty again.

"That's her, Mom. The cute one I was telling you about. I asked her if she was baby-sitting and she said, 'No, this is my two year old daughter. I was going to tell you about her but I thought it might blow your mind'."

"Is she married?" I asked in a concerned voice.'

"No, she didn't marry the baby's father. I feel so stupid, asking her if she was baby-sitting."

"You didn't know," I said reassuringly. Then I had a sudden thought. "Did you ask her for a date?"

"No, but I may," he said with a bit of defiance in his voice.

I wanted to shout at him, 'You can't! I won't let you!', but I didn't. That might have made him angry enough to do it to spite me, his bossy mother. It would have angered me if my parents had ordered me around when I was a know-it-all teenager many years ago.

After thinking for a moment, I said, "Are you prepared to take on the responsibility of a two year old child?"

"Mom, I'm not going to get serious about her. It's just a date."

"Just a date could lead to much more than you're prepared to handle right now. Think about it before you decide to ask her out."

He did, and he didn't ask her out. The following week he met another girl from another town. The next day I overheard him on the telephone talking to a family friend who lived in the new girl's town. He gave the new girl's name, then said, "Do you know her parents?"

You see! It is hereditary!

Our other son was seventeen when he met a pretty girl from out of town at a teen dance. "She was staring at me from across the room and we danced the rest of the evening," he said wonderingly. "She blew in my ear while we were dancing. I have a date with her next Saturday night."

Although the ear-blowing during a first evening dance nagged at me, I didn't say anything. I didn't even ask about her parents. He hadn't had a chance to meet them yet.

On Sunday morning after his date, I said, "Did you like her parents?"

"I didn't meet them," he replied. She had me pick her up at a friend's trailer on the edge of town. We have a date for next Saturday night."

"You said she's just fifteen years old. Tell her you want to meet her parents," his dad said.

After the second date and the third date, he had not met her parents. He was still picking her up and letting her off at the friend's trailer.

Finally, his father said, "If she doesn't take you to meet her parents this weekend, I want you to consider not dating her again. I don't like the situation. She's underage, and she hasn't introduced you to her family. Something bad might happen to her at the trailer and you could be blamed for it."

Again, after the fourth date, our son had not met her parents. "Well, son," his father said, "I'm not going to order you to stop dating her but, if you continue to date her, you will have to walk. I still have final control over the car."

Her pick-up trailer was thirty miles away, but our son didn't walk to it, and he didn't have to break a date. He had decided beforehand to not ask her out again. Apparently, he didn't like the situation either --- after thinking on his father's worries the week before.

The worries were not unfounded. Bad things did happen at that trailer a few months later, although the girl our son had dated was not publicly involved.

'Don't worry', my teenagers may say to me. 'Don't worry'. When I hear those 'reassuring words', my worrying tends to double or triple in strength. I've heard those words too many times before.

"Don't worry, Mom. She isn't that kind of girl."

What kind of girl does he mean? Now, I am worried.

"Don't worry, Mom. We've only gone steady for six months."

Six months? Has it been that long? Now, I am worried.

"Don't worry, Mom. I'm old enough to take care of myself."

He's just a teenager. Now, I am worried.

Is anyone ever old enough to take care of themselves?

When I was a teenager I was taught: anything worthwhile is worth waiting for. Today's society tends to teach: if it feels good, go ahead and do it.

No one seems to be any happier because of the change.

Don't worry. Don't worry. Don't worry, I remind myself and turn to the Lord in prayer.

"Don't worry about anything; instead, pray about everything. Tell God what you need, and thank him for all he has done.' (Philippians 4:6 NLT)

Parents need to build solid sexual standards for their children from infancy on by taking a firm stand. Don't back away from a child's questions on sex, but don't tell too much too soon --- or too little too late.

As for teenagers, offer full knowledge, express high moral standards, and live those standards in your life. Our shining example speaks much louder than words.

Love those teenagers.

Listen to them.

Pray for them.

Hold them close in your heart.

'The best and most beautiful things in the world cannot be seen or even touched – they must be felt with the heart.'   Helen Keller

Teenage Allergies to Household Chores

It's a fact. Most teenagers are allergic to household chores. Ask them to do something around the house and they will systematically develop 'I'll do it later' forgetfulness or sustain temporary deafness: "But Mom, we didn't hear you ask us to do that."

These unique allergy symptoms are often accompanied with nagging aches 'my head hurts', reoccurring drowsiness 'I'm awfully tired right now', and sudden pains 'my back's hurting for some reason'.

We discovered a simple cost-free cure for our teenage household allergies. We gave them a dose of logic called 'no work, no play'. If they didn't do their chores, they couldn't go out when their friends called for them.

The recovery rates were miraculous. It worked every time as long as we dished out an iron-will with a kind smile, and didn't let our sympathetic nature give in to any idle promises that they'd do their chores later if we would let them go out 'just this once' without doing their work first. Sometimes it would have been far easier for parents to do the household chores themselves, but lazy children can easily become lazy adults.

Negotiate through 'allergies' with a dose of kindness and a dose of respect.

Mowing the lawn was not one of our older son's favorite chores, and he put off doing it for as long as he dared. "The grass is too wet," he said. "I'll do it later."

"But it's three o'clock in the afternoon and the sun's been shining all day long," I replied. "Bad excuse, son."

"I'm out of gas for the mower. I'll get it later."

"When? After the sun goes down and it's dark outside?"

"I'll need to clean the mower before I use it again. I'll do it later."

"Please do it now, son. The exercise is good for you."

"Then why don't you do it, Mom?"

"Wrong answer! Show a little respect or I'll send you to your room."

He mowed the lawn.

As I stood at the kitchen window watching him work, I wondered what I would have done if he had still refused to mow the lawn. My teenage son was nine inches taller and thirty pounds heavier than me. I had not mentioned sending him to his room since he was seven, and then only occasionally when immediate action was necessary.

Later, I told his dad of my threat. "What if he had stood there and disobeyed me?" I asked. "He's too old, and too big to be sent to his room."

"You needn't worry," my husband said. "We all know you're a mean mama."

"That's not a very nice thing to say."

"Let me put it another way," he said. "He respects your authority. You're consistent. You're fair. You pitch in and help whenever you can."

"That sounds better than saying I'm a mean mama."

"You're that, too, but I meant it as a compliment."

I knew I had not handling my son's lawn mowing episode in the best way possible. Instead of issuing the 'go to your room' threat, I should have offered a logical consequence in a calm controlled voice. "Mow the lawn now, and I'll take you shopping at the mall later."

I had broken one of my own rules: Hold the words to 25 or less. Fewer words have a better chance of sinking in.

Negotiating kindly and respectfully with the 'consequences option' is a sure-fire cure for teenage allergies to household chores. In fact, it works for younger children, too.

Disciplining a child toward self-discipline is a long, slow process that takes a lot of patience and understanding on both sides. All children are unique individuals. We need to identify the uniqueness of each child's personality, make appropriate adjustments, and discipline them accordingly.

Our daughter, the oldest of three, was the shy one. When she was two, I said, "Pick up your toys or I'll throw them in the garbage." She hurried to obey.

Our older son, with 'the commander' personality, refused to pick up his toys at the age of two. When I threatened to throw the toys away, he went into his room and came out with more. "Let's throw <u>all</u> my toys away," he said. To stay in control of the situation, I followed through with my threat and threw his toys away. When he went to bed, I took his toys out of the garbage and stored them on a shelf in the garage. Two weeks later, I gave them back to him, and said, "Let's try again." After that, he picked up his toys when I asked him to.

Our younger son, the charmer, simply ignored me when I threatened to throw his toys away. I hid them and brought them back out two weeks later. He didn't care. He was too busy entertaining siblings and friends to worry about toys. Then I gave him the either/or option. "If you want to go with me, you have to pick up your toys first."

Because of his out-going, fun loving personality, he eagerly picked up every toy in the house if it meant he got to go somewhere afterwards.

Treat the teenage allergies with a heartfelt dose of love.

We need to often tell them we love them. No matter what personality we face when trying to cure those allergies to household chores, we should start with love. Show it with a warm smile, a tender touch, or a happy hug. Don't assume, as I did, that our child should know we love him because we say it with a kiss every night at bedtime.

I learned about the importance of saying 'I love you' long ago, when our older son was five and came home from morning kindergarten in a terrible mood. After I had reminded him several times to eat his lunch, he jumped up and ran outside. I waited a few minutes for him to return, then I went outside looking for him. I called out his name again and again, but he didn't answer. Then, just as I was about to ask a neighbor for help, my son stepped out from behind a shrub in the empty lot behind our house, and trudged home.

"Why didn't you answer me?" I asked.

"I was trying to run away," he said. "But I didn't know where to go."

Why was he trying to run away? I started to send him to his room for scaring me like that. I was upset, disappointed and hurt. I wanted to order him to stop being silly. Then I wanted to beg him to stay. But that would put him in charge and, the next time things didn't please him, he'd probably threaten to run away again.

So, I hid my fears and softly said, "If you're unhappy here, please pack a bag and I'll take you anywhere you want to go." (Perhaps that would make him realize that there's no place like home.)

But it didn't. "I'll get my clothes," he said.

I carried a small suitcase into his room and sat down on the bed, praying all the while for the right words to heal the rift between us. "Your dad and I will miss you, son" I said. "We love you very much."

"You love me," he cried, and wrapped his little arms around my neck. "I don't want to leave you."

As I hugged him tight, I thanked God for giving me those magic words, and I vowed to tell my children and my husband I loved them as often as possible.

Negotiate through 'teenage allergies' with lighthearted doses of laughter.

Kind laughter is an easy cure for 'teenage allergies', disagreements and family woes. Concentrate on developing everyone's sense of humor to have a happy home atmosphere. Keep adding new jokes to the joke jar and share them often. Here are a few to share.

For Avery's high school graduation, her parents gave her a compact car. Later, she was talking about it with a friend. "How many will it hold?" Her friend asked.

"It was designed to hold five passengers," Avery replied with a smile. "But if they all take turns holding their breath, we can get ten teenagers in there."

My Mom does bird imitations," said Ian. "She watches me like a hawk."

Josh asked Aaron, "Do you want to hear a really good Batman impression?

"Yes". Aaron said.

"Not the KRYPTONITE!" yelled Josh.

"That's Superman," Aaron said, shaking his head.

"Thanks, Man," Josh said. "I've been practicing."

Why are you so unhappy about the birthday present Uncle Orville sent you?" Sherry asked her teenage son.

"I remember him asking you whether you wanted a small check or a large check."

"Yes," said her son Drew, "but I didn't know he was talking about a tie."

Apparently, taking a day off is not something you should do when you work for a calendar company.

"What did the doctor tell you to do when you broke your leg in two places?"
"Quit going to those two places."

"What do you call a woman with one leg?"
"Eileen"

"Where does a one-legged woman work?"
"IHOP."

"What did the shark say after he ate the clownfish/"
"That tasted a little funny."

"What's the difference between a cat and a comma?"
"A cat has claws at the end of its paws. A comma is a pause at the end of its clause."

Being paid for doing some of the house chores was another remedy that seemed to ease those teenage allergies. We agreed to give out a set sum of money each week if their regular chores were done on time without any reminders from us. The agreement worked quite well.

We paid extra for chores beyond their expected daily routines. Our daughter started baby-sitting when she was thirteen and she apparently did a good job because she was soon flooded with baby-sitting requests. There were times when we wanted her to stay home with her younger brothers, who were then ten and seven, while we went out for the evening.

So we offered to pay her to baby-sit for us if she had a paying request somewhere else on the night we wanted her. These were her own rowdy brothers who loved to tease her, especially when we weren't around.

We decided to pay her every time she sat for us, and we offered our sons fifty-cents each if they were good for their sister. From that day forth they were always good for her. At least, they said they were good. We happily paid them the money if we didn't come home to any sibling arguments.

Our daughter was quite frugal with her money. She saved her baby-sitting money and her allowance auspiciously, and added to her savings account regularly.

When we went shopping for clothes, she always looked at the price tags first, even if Mom and Dad were paying the bill. If she was told she had to spend her own money, she didn't want to go shopping at all.

Our older son didn't deposit as much money in his savings account as his sister. His money-making position wasn't as good as hers. He didn't want to baby-sit. He wanted to mow lawns and by a lifeguard at outdoor pools. That was seasonal work where we lived.

As a pre-teen, our younger son was a little careless with his money. Did I say a little? He was a lot careless with it. He left quarters, dimes, nickels and pennies laying around in his room and all over the house. Once he absently tucked a five dollar bill into his hip pocket and promptly lost it. I was always laundering the dollar bills he left in his jeans. After warning him about his carelessness again and again, I finally said, "Give me all your money, son. When you want some of it, you will have to come to me".

Three days later, his grandfather came by and asked him to cut weeds out of the bean field. "I'll work for you, Grandpa," he said. "But you don't have to pay me. Mom takes all my money."

I hung my head. That remark sounded terrible, but true. So his banker Dad helped our son open a savings account at the bank downtown, and showed him how to deposit his money. But Dad did not show him how to make withdrawals,

As a teenager, our younger son learned how to handle his money well. He gathered and sold used golf balls, washed and polished cars, and worked at a golf club pro shop. He always added regularly to that savings account at the bank.

Parents need not be afraid to designate household chores. Teenagers aren't really allergic to them. They just seem to be until they're made to realize that work can be fun, especially when they learn that there will be no play until after the chores are done.

We have always encouraged our teenagers to find summer employment and odd jobs. One odd job they found was odd indeed. There was an old abandoned hotel above the bank where their father worked, and the owners hired our teenage sons to clean out the ancient rooms which had been used for storage by various people over the years. All of the windows had been boarded up or removed several years earlier. The only lights they had to work by were three bare bulbs hanging from the hallway ceilings. The many rooms were shadowed in darkness and filled with dusty, clinging cobwebs.

They carried flashlights up the stairs to shine in dark corners and they wore gloves to protect their hands from the fallen plaster and dead bird skeletons they had to carry out to the garbage.

"It is r-e-a-l scary working up there in the dark," they said.

Then we laughed about their vivid imaginations and fears.

At the end of the second day, they invited me up the rickety stairs to see the progress they had made in cleaning out the awful mess. So, I climbed the dark dingy stairs to praise their work. I should have known better.

It was dark. Very dark. My younger son gave me a flashlight and we cautiously walked from room to room, inspecting them. Finally he said, "Isn't it scary up here?"

"No," I said. "It's just dark. I'm not scared of the dark."

"Follow me back here," my older son said. "We want to show you something."

I followed him to the far end of the dark hall. We stopped at the open door to an even darker room.

"Shine the flashlight in there," he whispered, pointing to the darkened room. I did. The light fell on a long, dark rectangular box.

"What is it?" I asked.

"A wooden coffin."

"Oh," I said breathlessly, my anxious heart pounding in my throat. "How --- how did it get up here?"

"We don't know. We just found it."

"Is it empty?" I whispered.

"We don't know."

Suddenly a black hand reached out to take the flashlight from me.

I jumped and screamed!

Then I realized that the black-gloved hand belonged to my younger son. He wanted to take the flashlight in for a closer look. We all laughed at my frightened scream until we were breathless.

I had to agree with them. It was indeed scary up there.

It was fun working with those tantalizing teenagers whenever we could. Sharing a laugh and a smile while we were working together made the work fun. Happy times shared on the task made for fond, lasting memories. Such memories were priceless gifts to give to our children. The memories cannot be bought with money earned, nor can the togetherness by substituted with lavish gifts because we can't, or won't, take the time to GIVE the time.

We got to laugh with our teenagers more by working with them often. We let some of our presents to them be our presence.

Spending time together increases the happiness and harmony in any family. Add a little music and the harmony is complete.

The song *A Place in the Choir* written be Bill Staines is guaranteed to bring a smile to the face of even the grumpiest one in the group. The Celtic Thunder music video on YouTube features all the animals mentioned in the song. Two of the many stanzas are:

All God's creatures got a place in the choir
Some sing low and some sing higher.
Some sing out loud on a telephone wire.
Some just clap their hands,
or paws, or anything they've got now
It's a simple song a little song everywhere
By the ox and the fox and the grizzly bear,
The dopey alligator and the hawk above,
The sly old weasel and the turtle dove.

Enjoy the song together and joyfully negotiate through teenage allergies to household chores with double doses of kindness, respect, laughter and love.

'Love one another ---'(John 15:12a NASB)

The Case of the Missing Athletic Supporter

Fairly athletic teenagers who decide to participate in organized sports programs and subject themselves to possible failures and frustrations need to know that their parents are with them to support and sustain them through the good times and the bad times.

Parents should be there, even if their teenagers sit on the bench and seldom get to participate in the game --- especially if their teenagers sit on the bench.

We need to show them that we care. We can't stay way because we're too busy, or too tired, or can't tolerate their disappointments. Our children need us.

We can't be a missing athletic supporter. A missing athletic supporter is useless; it doesn't help to comfort or uplift anything.

I didn't want to be a missing athletic supporter. I was there when our younger son suffered a slight concussion in the freshman football game. His father, who had played football on a championship team in high school, always said to me, ""If one of the boys gets hurt in a game, don't run down to the field to see about him. Let the coaches and trainers take care of his injury. They know what to do."

I didn't run down to the field when our son staggered to the sidelines, obviously in confusion. I couldn't leave his dad. I was too busy holding him back. He wanted to run down to the field to see about our ailing son.

I was there during a sophomore basketball game when our older son sat on the bench until the last thirty

73

seconds of the game. Our team was ahead by twenty-five points throughout most of the game and the other eight players on our team had been substituted into the game at regular intervals from the first quarter on.

I hurt for our son sitting there and not getting a chance to play. My stomach was tied in knots for him. He was not an outstanding player, but he was as good as some of the others, and he had not missed any practices or disobeyed the coach. Why wasn't he getting a few minutes of playing time?

What was the coach thinking?

When we picked him up after the game, our son hung his head and said, "I asked my coach why I didn't get to play a little bit, and he said I wasn't good enough. I want to quit the team."

His father and I were shocked. Our son had played basketball since the fourth grade and he had suffered with disappointments before, but he had always played at some point during the game. He was fast. He was quick. He had never considered quitting the team. He must have misunderstood his coach's cruelly blunt remark. "Don't quit in haste," his father said. "Give yourself the weekend to think it over."

On Monday morning, after a thoughtful weekend, our son said, "I'm turning in my uniform today."

I sighed. "We hate to see you do it, but it's your decision to make. Why don't you talk to the coach again before you quit the team?"

He said he would and, as he left for school, my spirits lifted. The coach would surely ask him to finish out the year with the season almost over, and would convince him that every man was needed on the team.

They didn't have enough students out for varsity basketball team as it was, and at the sophomore level, building better players was the main objective of the game.

I was wrong again. When our son handed over his uniform and said, "I'm quitting," the unconcerned coach said, "Okay, you weren't going to make a living playing basketball anyway," and he walked away.

What was the coach thinking?

I wish I could say that something good had come out of our son's sad separation from his high school basketball team. But it didn't happen that year. He went out for track the next day, ran on concrete floors because the weather was too cold to practice outside, and developed shin splints in both legs. Even with the ever-present pain, he had a good track season, but he did not reach his personal goals in the sprint competitions.

The basketball team lost their last three tournament games. Teammates came down with bouts of flu and they took turns missing the games. On the first night, the team dressed just five players and for the last two games, there were only six that didn't have the flu.

The world will never know if our son would have played in one of those games, even if he had stayed on the team. But the coach was right about one thing. Our son did not become a professional basketball player.

The next year was better for our son. He didn't bother with basketball after finishing a successful football season. He worked out on the weights instead and later won the 'most dedicated weight-lifter' award at school.

He went out for track in the spring and had an excellent season, surpassing all of his earlier expectations. We were there to support his endeavors all the way.

'We can rejoice, too, when we run into problems and trials, for we know that they help us develop endurance. And endurance develops strength of character, and character strengthens our confident hope of salvation.' (Romans 5:3-4 NLT)

Our older son's junior year on the high school's football squad ended on a very positive note for him. He was the second string running back and, due to another's unfortunate injury, he was placed in the starting line-up for the last three games of the season. H gained over 100 yards each game and scored two winning touchdowns. He was eagerly anticipating his senior year in football when he would be in the offensive starting line-up from the first game on.

Then the football coach left for another job, and the school hired a new one. He didn't like the way our son ran with the ball, and he moved him to the defensive back position for the season. Our son did the role assigned to him, then stood on the sideline during the team's offensive plays, watching someone else carry the ball.

I sat in the stands and wondered what the coach was thinking. We weren't scoring enough touchdowns to win. At the end of the season, I gave a sigh of relief. "I'm glad it is over," I said to our son.

My son nodded in agreement.

"Was it worth all your frustrations?"

"Yes," he said. "My teammates stood by me, encouraging me all the way. They sympathized with my position. They're good friends. And I learned something about myself."

"What's that?"

"I can take just about any disappointment and keep on going."

Perhaps there ARE good lessons to be learned from competitive sports. We need to search for them with positive attitudes, even in the most unpleasant circumstances, even in the failures.

Learning to lose is just as important as learning to win. We can all look at failure to win as a small setback toward long-term goals. We can see failure as a way to develop positive attitudes by recognizing that we can choose how we react to setbacks.

Don't blame others.

Don't dwell on self-doubts.

Do take action by choosing to take on new challenges.

Develop an attitude of gratitude.
Choose to be happy.
Choose to make someone else happy.

"The setbacks, mistakes, miscalculations, and failures we have shoved out of our children's way are the very experiences that teach them how to be resourceful, persistent, innovative, and resilient citizens of the world." Jessica Lahey from *The Gift of Failure*

Our younger son went out for football a second year under the new coach. He saw very little playing time on the field. He was tall and thin, maturing later than his shorter, solidly built classmates. The coach told him he couldn't play him because he lacked experience. And he lacked experience because he didn't get much playing time. It was an endless circle with no room for improvement.

The next fall, our son joined the school's golf team instead of the football team. He competed well throughout the season, qualified for the sectional competition and was later elected captain of the team. His athletic abilities seemed to lean toward the swinging sport of golf. He had made a wise choice.

Our lives would be quite boring if God were to give all of us the same abilities to do the same things well. We need to seek out our own special talents and work with them to excel with hope, happiness, and faith.

What is faith? It is the confident assurance that something good is going to happen. It is the certainty that what we hope for is waiting for us, even though we cannot see it up ahead.

'Faith shows the reality of what we hope for,
it is the evidence of things we cannot see.'
(Hebrews 11:1 NLT)

Our younger son began playing basketball at school in the fourth grade. He was usually on the second string, spending much of his time sitting on the bench cheering on his teammates. He liked basketball and he stayed with it year after year, practicing faithfully to improve his skills. Year after year, he was the second man on the second team, averaging about one quarter a game playing time if he was lucky. But he wanted more. And he had faith.

He was confident that something good was going to happen, if he worked at it hard enough. All he had to do was prove himself to his coach. Then it happened during his senior year, in the high school's varsity game. A starting player hurt his hand in practice and another twisted his ankle. The coach placed our son in the starting line-up.

He was a nervous wreck at home before the game. He couldn't eat. He couldn't sit still. After all these years of faithful practice, he was in the starting line-up.

We were there when they introduced him over the loud speaker and he ran out onto the floor with the other four.

By the end of the first quarter the score was zero for the visiting team and thirteen points for our son. He could not miss a shot, so his teammates kept passing him the ball to shoot

The crowd roared. They loved it and gave him a standing ovation at the end of the first quarter. The team later won the game. It was a bench-warmer's dream come true.

Three games later, the injured players were back in the starting line-up and our son was back on the bench. He had played well, but being a second-stringer was his role. For the rest of the season he practiced hard to improve his skills, and he kept the faith, even though sitting on the bench part of the time was harder than ever before. He knew he could play as good as anyone on the floor. He had proven it.

The surprise ending to this story was when the end of the season arrived the team was the best in the area and a local paper featured the starting team in the newspaper, complete with individual photos and write-ups. The coach announced, "We have a starting six line-up this year, not a starting five." And he included our son in the feature article.

What was the coach thinking?

My husband and I attended every sports event. We were not the missing athletic supporters. But I definitely was the prime suspect in the case of a missing athletic supporter.

With teenagers in sports and other activities, there was a lot of laundry time for me. I washed, dried, folded and divided the laundry for them to take to their rooms and store in the appropriate drawers. It was an ongoing process.

One day, I was sitting at the kitchen table. My son ran to me, shouting, "Where is my athletic supporter. I need it now. I'm late!"

"Isn't it in your drawer?" I asked.

Suddenly everything went black.

I was blinded by a missing athletic supporter. My other son had sneaked up behind me and put it over my head.

Both boys doubled over with laughter.

When they finally caught their breath, one of them said, "From now on, one ends up on your head every time you put both athletic supporters in only one drawer pile."

I had to laugh with them. It was a funny penalty.

Humor is the harmony of the heart. If loved ones in your family seem a little sad, try cheering them up with some 'jar jokes' that pertain to sports.

Why did the golfer wear two pairs of pants?
In case he got a hole in one.

Betty recently stumbled upon her favorite new sports team. It's a woman's bowling squad called *I Can't Believe it's Not Gutter.*

Blood may be thicker than water, but baseball beats them both. Jen learned this after explaining to her two boys that they were half-French on their father's side, and half-Yankee, meaning that their other set of parents came from an old new England family.

Her younger son looked worried. "But we're still one hundred percent Red Sox. Right, Mom?"

As a high school football coach, James was aware that student athletes often focused too much on sports. He told of one such player who tried to call him at home one night.

"He's not here," his wife said.

The lad became frantic and said, "I have to speak to coach right away."

"Just calm down please and I'll have him call you as soon as he gets home," James's wife said. "What's your number?"

The flustered lad said, "Three."

Callie's son was upset that his baseball coach yelled whenever he or a teammate made a mistake.

That's just something coaches do," Callie said. "It isn't personal."

"If it isn't personal, why does he use my name?" asked her son.

A set of golf clubs walked into a bar.

"What'll you have?" Asked the bartender.

"Nothing for me," said one of the clubs. "I'm the driver.

What ae you doing this weekend?" Asked Miles.

"I'm going to buy glasses," said Giles.

"And then what?" Asked Miles.

"Then we'll see."

What did the football coach say to the broken vending machine?

"Give me my quarterback."

Our daughter didn't participate in high school sports but she was an avid fan of those who did. She was dedicated to group activities that didn't draw much attention to her individually. She played clarinet in band and marimba in both pep band and jazz band. She took part in scholastic bowl, Girl Scouts and 4-H. She learned to be an outstanding cook, seamstress and needlework artist.

But as her brother prepared for high school, he decided that wasn't enough. ""I want you to go out for cheerleader. I want a sister who does lots of things in high school," he said.

"Oh no," she said shaking her head. "I'm not trying out for cheerleader."

"Then how about the Pom-Pom squad?"

"I suppose I could try out for that," she replied.

So she did. She knew music. She could dance. She could be available to perform at half-time during basketball games. She worked hard, practicing a dance routine for try-outs.

On the day of try-outs after school, I anxiously waited for her to come home with the results. I had even practiced saying, "I'm so proud of you for trying."

Both boys burst through the kitchen door before I even knew she was home. "She got it! She got a place on the Pom-Pom squad," they yelled.

"I wanted to tell Mom first," she said, walking in with a smile on her face.

I hugged her and said, "I'm so proud of you for trying."

After that, she tried out for the flag team in band and was chosen to perform. She had a great senior year, and her brother was glad he had an older sister who did lots of things in high school.

We may be disappointed if we fail, but we are doomed if we don't try.

If there's some tension among siblings in the family for one reason or another, a musical quiz about sports may help restore harmony and laughter.

Question: What is the theme song for Boston Red Sox baseball team?

Answer: *Sweet Caroline* since 2002. It was written and performed by Neil Diamond in 1969. He was thinking of Caroline Kennedy (President John Kennedy's daughter) when he wrote it. Some of the lyrics are:

Hands, touching hands
Reaching out, touching me, touching you
Sweet Caroline
Good times never seemed so good
I've been inclined
To believe they never would
But now I look at the night and I don't seem so lonely ---

During the COVID19 Pandemic, Neil Diamond changed the words to:

Hands, washing hands
Reaching out, don't touch me, I won't touch you
Sweet Caroline -------

Question: What is the Atlanta Braves baseball team theme song?

Answer: *Tomahawk Chop* since 1991.

Question: What do archrivals Chicago Cubs and St. Louis Cardinals have in common?

Answer: Same theme song *Take Me out to the Ballgame*

During the COVID19 virus their theme song words were changed to:

Keep me home from the ballgame
Keep me out of the crowd.
Buy me some TP and face masks,
I sure wish baseball was back.
I'll still root, root, root for the Cardinals/Cubbies.
If they don't win it's a shame.
Is it one? Two? Three months
We'll wait for the old Ball Game?

Questions: What is the New York Yankees victory song?
Answer: *New York, New York* sung by Frank Sinatra

Question: What other sports event uses the *New York, New York* theme song?
Answer: The Belmont Stakes, one of horse racing's Triple Crown events.

Question: What is the theme song for the Preakness race in Baltimore, Maryland?
Answer: *Maryland, My Maryland*

Question: What is the theme song for the Kentucky Derby horse race Crown?
Answer: *My Old Kentucky Home*

When our sons were much younger and their dad coached their little league baseball teams, I was there to see the outfielders in their usual positions. The right fielder was tracking airplanes in the sky. The left fielder was watching people walk by. And our son, the center fielder was drawing pictures in the dirt.

Later, when our son took his turn at bat, he hit a ball past the pitcher. He ran to first base and safely jumped on the bag with both feet. "Hey, Mom," he yelled, waving at me in the stands. "Look! I made it!"

I cheered loud and long for his success.

After five innings, the game ended with our team losing five runs to the other team's nine runs. I silently practiced a pep talk for my son and his dad to ease their disappointment. But I soon learned that they didn't need a pep talk.

"We lost," my son said to me. "But Dad said not to worry. We were good sports and played a good game. I like baseball."

We should never be that missing athletic supporter --- even for our very young player. We should always follow these five B-attitudes:

Be ready to cheer for the team, win or lose.
Be encouraging, not discouraging.
Be quiet if you can't be constructive.
Be prepared ---bring bubble gum for the team.
BE THERE. Show them that you care.

After watching a pee-wee basketball game, my husband gave his eight year old son some fatherly coaching advice. "Son, don't stop to pull up your socks during a fast break. It kind of slows down the play."

In the spring of his seventh grade, our older son went out for track competition at school. He had just celebrated his thirteenth birthday and, because he was five foot six inches he was the only seventh grader placed on the heavyweight (or eighth grade) team. When he came home and told me, I shook my head. How could he be a one-hundred-two pound heavyweight?

"Coach wants me to run the mile," he said. "I don't want to, but Coach says I can do it, so I guess I'll give it a try."

He competed in the mile race all season long, cut 35 seconds off his time, and placed fifth at the district meet.

After the district competition, he was allowed to compete with other seventh graders at the County Meet. Coach entered him in the 400 meter race for the first time. His dad ran that race during his track days, and before the big race, he gave our son a few words of advice. "Get in the lead fast. Hold it until the far turn. Make the other runners push to catch you. Then give it all you've got in the home stretch."

His dad sat with me in the bleachers and the race began. Our son followed dear old dad's first directions correctly. He was in the lead on the back stretch. "I can't stand it," his dad whispered. "This is worse than running it myself. My stomach's in knots. I can't get my breath. Will he have anything left for the home stretch?"

He did. He won his heat. The final results placed him second at the County Meet. I was glad the race was only once around the track. If it had been any longer, his dad would not have had anything left to watch the home stretch.

Our younger son went out for track in school and had to stay in the long distance races, running the mile and two-mile at every meet. He stayed with the rigorous routine and complained about it only once. It was just before the fifth meet in as many days. "I wish I could run fast like my brother," he said wistfully. "Those short races look a lot easier than the ones I have to run."

Later, after his older brother graduated, we learned to our surprise that he COULD run fast like his brother. He just didn't want to compete against him.

We also discovered he was a talented triple-jumper in track. He won his event and racked up lots of points for his track team as an upperclassman. He iced his knees after the triple jump events. And his left one was really bothering him during the district competition his senior year. He had bandaged it carefully before his event. On the first run-through, his knee buckled beneath him. He fell face first into the sandpit.

We looked at his knee and instantly knew he would not be competing in triple jump any time soon. His track competition days were over. He wasn't going to reach his expectations, his hopes, or his dreams for the season.

He limped over and stood between his father and me. We cheered his teammate on to a second place medal. Our son helped and encouraged his teammate all the way, talking after each jump, and sharing pointers for greater distances. And all the while, we stood by him.

We did not discuss his injury. It was too raw right then. He was hurting in his heart far more than he was hurting in his knee. That was a pain for families to share in private at home. All we could do at the meet was stand by him and support him through his acute disappointment.

At the end of the meet, he called to a teammate, "What triple jump distance won first place?"

"Don't ask," I warned him. But it was too late.

The teammate told him the distance. Later he said, "You were right, Mom. I shouldn't have asked. Just one good jump and I would have won that event."

He made it through with his positive attitude and good sense-of-humor bounce-back. And he commiserated with several other injured, disappointed athletes on the team.

We should praise the Lord in all things, and look to the good, even in the most disappointing situations. We need God's guidance to wisely help our teenagers through any competitive sports situations.

We can celebrate the harmony of sports programs with these three victory-related songs:

We are the Champions of the World and *We will Rock You* were both performed by Queen and written by Freddie Mercury in 1977.

God Bless America was written by Irving Berlin during World War 1 in 1918

Don't become a useless, worn-out, missing athletic supporter. Be there for your daughters. Be there for your sons.

'Tough times never last. Tough people do.
Robert Schuller

Who's in Charge Here?

Who's in charge here, when it comes to teenagers and household clothes?

We used to have children who woke up at the beginning of the day, kissed us, and said, "Good morning, Mommy and Daddy."

Then they became teenagers who woke up at the beginning of the day, ran to the kitchen and said, "I'm hungry. What's to eat?"

We used to have children who came home from school, hugged us, and said, "I missed you, Mommy and Daddy".

Then they became teenagers who came home after school, dashed for the kitchen, and said, "I'm hungry. What's to eat?"

We used to have children who came to one of us after dinner, and said, "Read to me."

Then they became teenagers who came to us after dinner, looked to the kitchen and said, "I'm hungry. What's to eat?"

Could those teenagers really be the toddlers we had to coax to eat? Could they really be the little tots we made funny faces for, and whey they laughed, we shoveled in the food they didn't want to eat? Could they really be the preschoolers who merely picked at the food on their plates?

Yes, yes, and yes. It was hard to believe, but we were there when the metamorphoses transpired. Almost overnight, their newfound hunger hit us unaware, unprepared, and unequipped. Before teenagers, our refrigerator and pantry doors were closed and the shelves inside were filled with food that sometimes grew stale and had to be thrown away. Then our kids became hungry teenagers, and they took turns hanging on open doors, waiting for me to line the empty shelves with food for them to eat before the day was done.

I tried reading articles and book on how to feed a hungry family for less, but their plans just did not work for us. If I had served green pepper slices for a snack or one-half a peanut butter sandwich for a meal, our famished clan might have turned me into the authorities for child neglect and appetite abuse.

One Tuesday, when our children were in high school, my husband finished lunch and asked me, "What's for dinner?"

"Chip-coated chicken," I replied.

"Good. I like that," he said.

He went back to work and I went to the store, bought a twin bag of potato chips, brought it home and set it on the pantry shelf.

That evening at dinner, my husband said, "Baked chicken? I had my mouth all set for chip-coated chicken."

"I know," I said, and hung my head. "Someone ate all the chips after school before I could get them on the chicken."

The next day at breakfast, I said to my husband, "Would you like a cherry delight dessert tonight?"

"I'd love it," he said. "You haven't fixed that in a long time."

I went to the store, bought a box of graham crackers for crust, brought it home and set it on the pantry shelf.

After dinner, he said, "Everything was good, but I saved room for cherry delight. I thought about it all day long. Bring on the dessert."

"No dessert," I said, and hung my head. "Someone ate all the graham crackers before I could crush them into crust."

To appease his disappointment, I suggested banana pudding for the next night. "That would taste good," he said in a doubtful voice.

The next morning, I want to the store, bought the bananas, brought them home, and hid them behind the bread box.

That night, my husband's eyes searched the dinner table then, with fear in his voice, he asked, "Where's the banana pudding? I've been counting on it all day."

I had to look away as I said, "Some 'monkeys' found my hiding place and ate all the bananas." I couldn't stand to see a grown man cry because we 'had no bananas today'. Oh no, that was the title of a song by Frank Silver and Irving Cohn published in 1923.

"Yes, we have no bananas
We have no bananas today
We've string beans, and onions
Cabbages, and scallions
And all sorts of fruit and say
We have an old fashioned to-mah-to
A Long Island po-tah-to
But yes, we have no bananas
We have no bananas today."

We had to find a quick solution to maintain the harmony and happiness in our house. The answer was post-it notes on the food. Orange meant STOP! Do not eat this food. It is spoken for. Yellow with a name on it meant the food had been claimed by someone in the family. No note meant enjoy!

Three good thing immerged from all the teenage hunger.

One, we wanted our teenagers around the table at dinner, and we were able to get them there, as long as we served the food they liked.

Two, when they were younger and not so hungry before dinner, they said, 'May we help?' and no matter what I suggested, they replied, "Oh, I don't want to do THAT'. When they became hungry teenagers and I suggested setting the table, putting ice in the glasses or pouring the drinks, and they started to say, 'I don't want to ---', I quickly added, "If everyone helps, we'll be eating dinner sooner." And they all rushed about helping out.

Three, sharing jokes and laughter at the dinner table was a joy!

"I wrote a song about a tortilla."
"Actually, it's more of a wrap."

"Did you hear the one about the greedy peanut butter?"
"No."
"I'm not telling you. You might spread it."

"What do you call two cows that don't make milk?"
"Milk Dud and Udder Failure".

"What do you call a camel with no hump?"
"Humphrey"

A rancher was persuaded to cross-breed his cattle with hyenas. It was a disaster. The off- springs were the laughing stock of the community.

Who's in charge here when it comes to teenagers' household clothes? As a parent, I knew I should not try to limit my teenagers to my ancient view of appropriate clothing for all occasions. But this was not an easy thing to do. Thanks to the clothes-conscious teenagers in our house, I developed the blue denim blues.

It started when our teenagers became obsessed with brand name jeans in stonewashed, whitewashed, or acid washed hues. Those words didn't even exist when I was a teenager --- way back in the dark denim ages when blue was truly blue and no other color would do. If my jeans were faded as light as those expensive ones our teenagers wanted to buy, I called them worn-out and threw them away.

Heaven help me if I happened to throw away a too-tight, faded, ragged pair of jeans with rips in the thighs, holes at the knees, frayed hems, and seats worn thin.

"How could you, Mother?" Wailed one teenager or the other. "That was my favorite pair. Now, I don't have a decent thing to wear!"

One of our sons who wouldn't THINK of using the same towel twice before it was washed, frantically dashed through the house one morning in his briefs (denim-colored, of course) "I can't find my new jeans," he said with fear in his voice.

"Do you mean the pair you wore until late last night, and the day before that, and the day before that?" I asked.

"Yes!"

"They're standing alone in the laundry room waiting to be washed." As he headed for the laundry room, I shouted, "Don't you dare! They have to be washed today before the Board of Health gets 'wind' of them. Wear another pair."

We didn't always agree with our teenagers on the way they wanted to dress and they didn't always agree with us on the way we wanted to dress. But that was exactly what we expected with the generation gap in our household.

The art of being wise parents was knowing what to overlook. Disagreeing with our teenagers didn't mean that we were not being good parents. And we didn't want to feel guilty about the disagreements, or make our teenagers feel guilty about them either. But everyone in the family needed to hold back the anger and calmly listen to one another in order to think things through to an acceptable solution. After all, thinking for themselves is one of the things we wanted our teenagers to do in adulthood, and, as we had to help them along with their first faltering baby steps, we had to help them along with their first faltering adult-thinking steps, too.

We hoped and prayed that our teenagers would become self-confident enough to form their own opinions without being influenced by their peers or by other interfering adults. As we saw them exercising this newfound individuality, we remembered to respect their differing points of view. In return, they considered our views, too. Then, with consideration and kindness on both sides, we were able to work things out. Kindness is becoming at any age --- even between parents and teenagers, especially between parents and teenagers. It's simply another example of living by the Golden Rule that's been around for a long, long time.

But the Golden Rule is of no use to us whatsoever, unless we realize that it is our move, that our actions will always speak louder than words for closeness in the family, and so much of what is great has come from the closeness of strong family ties.

With that in mind I bought my husband a pair of the new, faded-blue denim jeans to wear so he would be in tune with his teenage children's latest craze. "They look like they've been worn before," he said. "Did you buy them at a thrift shop?"

"Silly Dad," I replied. "It's the latest trend. Just ask your kids. Now, get out of your old Dockers and try them on."

The faded jeans were too small by far. He couldn't zip them up at all. "What size are they?" He asked, as he sucked in his stomach for a smaller waist.

"Thirty-six. Your usual size, but the tag says 'trim and fit'. That must not be you. I'll exchange them for a 'regular' pair."

The 36 regular pair had a lot more room. In fact, there was enough room in those faded jeans for me to join him there.

"Now what'll I do," he said as he slumped into his favorite chair. "I'm not trim, or fit, or regular. I feel awful. I don't have a decent thing to wear."

That's when I knew ---- The blue denim blues were contagious. He had caught them too!

All he needed to do to survive those 'denim blues' was wear a smile. Nothing he wore would ever look as good as a friendly smile on his face.

We didn't mind seeing our teenagers in various shades of blue denim jeans, but we DID mind seeing them with the 'blues'. We wanted them to be happy, to have fun, and to enjoy the freedom of maturing adults. But with their freedom came the responsibility to think wisely or suffer the consequences. If that freedom was abused, it was our duty as parents to temporarily take it away.

We wanted to be friends with our teenagers, sharing in their triumphs and confidences, but we had to be parents first --- which meant enforcing the family rules, even when it gave us pain to do it.

Our rules were few, but firm. We wanted to know our teenagers' plans for the evening and we expected them home by midnight, unless other arrangements had been made with us beforehand. If they realized that they were going to be late, a considerate telephone call would do to ease our worries, because they knew we would not sleep soundly until they were home safe.

But if they were late without warning, they would be grounded one day for each minute after midnight. It was their responsibility to be on time to assure their freedom in the future.

"Other kids get to stay out after midnight," they said.

"Our reply was, "What do you need to do after midnight that you can't do before --- except get into late-night trouble?"

They didn't have an answer for that.

We insisted on no unchaperoned parties; and no taking drugs and alcohol.

Who's in charge here? The parents. We were negotiable on several issues, but ultimately we were still in charge.

Perhaps the most difficult part was giving our teenagers the freedom to make mistakes. When we saw them heading for difficulty and unhappy disappointments with unreliable friends, it was hard to let them make their own decisions. But they had to be free to fail.

Although we knew those situations would help them grow into mature adults, their failures could actually hurt us as much as, if not more than, them. Their state of happiness for the moment would be lost and they would be faced with 'beating their own case of the blues', but their lasting trait of happiness was directly linked with a teenager's freedom to make the choices

Thinking back to our own teenage years, we knew that we learned more from our failures than from our successes. And they would learn much from theirs, too.

We asked our teenagers to be honest and trustworthy, to keep up the family reputation. If they made a mistake or did something wrong, they were to come and tell us right away.

"But you will be mad," they said.

"Probably, but not as mad as we'll be if we hear it from someone else before we hear it from you." Teenagers do not want pals, patsies or pushovers for parents. They want parents who are willing to take the time to listen, even as they are fascinating us with adult wisdom one minute, and frustrating us with irrational demands the next; or charming us with responsible words one minute, and provoking us with brainless banter the next.

Parental sanity is saved when we remember that those ever-changing moods in our teenagers are not unusual. They are just being normal kids, searching for new identities, questioning parental authority, and experiencing rapid body changes.

After a trying day at home, if we find ourselves living with rebellious teenagers and not liking it very much, we should remember this: LOVE THEM TODAY. WE COULD LOSE THEM TOMORROW.

That sobering thought reminded me what was really important, restored my sense of humor, and renewed my strong allegiance with God.

Kindness is love in action. Show kindness to those teenagers with a comforting hug, a supportive smile, and a helping hand when they may need it the most –but expect it the least.

Never forget kindness.

Dizzy Drivers at the Wheel

Teaching teenagers to drive made this parent dizzy. It may well be one of the most traumatizing parental experiences know to woman or man.

When our daughter was fifteen and in the driver's education class at school, she earned the learner's permit allowing her to drive with a licensed parent or guardian. That turned out to be me. Her father was not up to the challenge. He said his nerves couldn't take it. I soon learned how wise he was. But our daughter needed driving experience. We couldn't turn her loose on an unsuspecting world if she didn't get a lot of practice driving before she turned sixteen. And she couldn't drive the car unless I rode along in the passenger's seat beside her. She was overjoyed every time I let her drive me around town, and I was filled with a sense of fear,

One day, in the high school parking lot, I backed the car into a parking space to wait for our permit-driving daughter. I thought it would be safer to let her drive forward rather than back out of the parking space.

When the dismissal bell rang, she ran out of the school, jumped in behind the wheel, and started the engine. She waved to some of her friends, honked the horn at others, jerked the car into reverse and started to back up.

"Stop!" I shouted.

Just in time, she slammed on the brakes.

Our back bumper was barely missing the front bumper of the car parked behind us. She had remembered that she was driving, and that the car was in a parking space, but she had forgotten to notice that it was facing OUT, not in.

The first few trips with my daughter driving were uneventful. She was evolving into a good, responsible driver.

Then came the winter's ice and snow. Thinking that she needed experience driving on the slippery roads, I gave her the keys and said, "Do you want to drive me to the grocery store?"

She did, of course. We climbed into the car and she casually drove onto the snow-covered road, tapping her fingers to the beat of the loud music on the car radio.

Two hundred feet north of our driveway, the car's tires hit a patch of ice and started to slide. "Lightly tap your brakes," I said.

She did, and the car went into a skid. Another car appeared, meeting up on the left, and a utility pole was waiting for us on the right. I panicked. I didn't tell her to turn the steering wheel in the direction of the skid, and I didn't remember to tell her to take her foot off the brake. I slammed my feet against imaginary brakes in the floorboard on the passenger side and yelled, "Stop! Stop! Stop!"

Of course, she could not stop the car. It was helplessly sliding about on the ice. It slid into the right-hand ditch, buried two tires in the snow, and stopped less than six inches from the utility pole.

Three teenage boys riding in the oncoming car jumped out and, in a few minutes, had our car out of the snow and back on the road again. We thanked the boys as they left.

"Mom, you drive," my daughter said. "I'm so embarrassed and my knees are shaking."

I smiled at her and said, "Nope. Get behind the wheel. My knees are shaking, too, but I've slid into ditches before and I'm still driving. You've got this."

She got behind the wheel and did a fine job chauffeuring me around on the ice and snow the rest of the trip.

After she received her driver's license on her sixteenth birthday, I wasn't required to ride in the passenger seat beside her. But I was apparently required to worry about her until she drove safely home at the end of the day. Parents were supposed to do that. It was an unwritten law.

Our son turned fifteen and soon was a permit-toting driver. I sat in the passenger seat beside him and spoke a running monologue, as I had done with his sister before him. "The stop light ahead turned red," I said.

"I know," he replied.

"Don't forget to turn on turning signal." I reminded him.

"I know," he said with an irritated edge in his voice.

"That car two blocks ahead of us is slowing down. Be prepared to stop," I warned him.

"I know, Mom," he snapped. "Why do you keep telling me things when I'm behind the wheel? Don't you trust my driving?"

I didn't. Not yet. But I couldn't tell him that. We were trying to build his driving confidence, not destroy it. So, I told him another truth instead. "Son, I know you know what you're doing, but I don't know when you're going to do it. That makes me a little anxious and when I'm a little anxious I sometimes talk too much. So, if you want to keep on driving, I guess you'll just have to let me keep on talking."

He keep on driving and, although I tried to curb it a little bit, I kept on talking.

Actually. He shouldn't have objected to my talking in the first place because turn-about is fair play. For years, I had listened to constant talking from the kids while I drove them about in the family car.

"Mother! Don't smooth down your hair when you're driving. Keep both hands on the wheel."

"Mom, you're going 40 again and the speed limit's 35."

"Mom, you missed the turn-off."

"Where?"

"About a mile back."

"Why didn't you tell me?"

Our daughter shrugged her shoulders. "I thought you knew what you were doing."

"Don't ever make that mistake again," I warned her. "With kids in the car I never know what I'm doing."

I was driving along and, from the back seat, my son said, "Stop the car, Mom. My cap just blew out the window."

"Hey, Mom. That man's waving at you."

"Where? I don't see anyone waving," I said from the driver's seat.

"He's right behind us with flashing red lights on the top of his car."

Wasn't that just great?

A female-driven car pulled out in front of us. Luckily, I missed her. "That's a woman driver for you," complained one of our sons.

"Yeah," agreed the other son. "You have to watch out for all women drivers. They're a crazy bunch."

"Wait a minute, boys," I said. "If you feel that way about women drivers, why do you let me drive you everywhere? I'll just quit. You can walk from now on."

"We don't mean you, Mom," they said. "We don't think of YOU as a woman driver."

Was that or was that not a dubious compliment? I still don't know if my sons don't think of me as a woman, or as a driver.

If the kids didn't give me words of advice while I drove them around, they offered 'visual aids'. "Hey, Mom," said my younger son. "Look at my latest drawing. Look! Look!"

"I can't look now, son. I have to watch where I'm driving the car."

"You aren't interested in my drawing."

"Yes I am," I said with a sigh. "All right, hold it up so I can see it in the rearview mirror. Ahhh --- yes. That's as nice drawwwwww ----- Oh, no! I almost hit the garbage truck parked in the middle of the road

99

because I was trying to see your drawing in the rearview mirror."

"Wow, Mom. Look at that girl on the sidewalk," said my son as I was driving him to basketball practice.

I couldn't look at her. I was meeting a slow-moving street sweeper.

"You didn't look," he said in a disappointed voice. "You don't care about the girl I'm going to ask out on a date."

Don't Care? Of course, I care!

Our dear daughter spoke up in the back seat. "Mom, I just cut my finger on the door handle. It's bleeding real bad. Here, look at it."

I couldn't look. I was about to side-swipe the automatic car wash entrance.

Her feelings were hurt, along with her bleeding finger. "You don't care," she sobbed. "I may be bleeding to death and you don't care."

Of course, I care! But how could I immediately tend to her finger when I was automatically washing the car?

I was driving the car, and for once, the three kids in the back seat were quiet. Suddenly, two hands covered my eyes, blinding me, and a teenager's voice said, "Hey, Mom. Guess who!"

I couldn't guess who it was, and I couldn't guess where the car was going.

When the teenagers tired of 'visual aids' for their driving mother, they turned to their typical 'automotive arguments'.

"Mom, please turn to another radio station," said our daughter.

"No. I like this station," said her brother.

"Too bad," she said. "I don't. Please find another station, Mom."

"No," he said. "Don't touch that dial."

"Yes."

"No."

After a continuous flow of 'yes' and 'no', I turned off the radio.

"Why did you do that?" They asked in unison.

"You two weren't listening to it," I said. "And I couldn't hear it above all your arguing. Now you have nothing to argue about --- until you think of something else."

There was harmony in the car when they calmly discussed and decided on the music to listen to.

One of the today's teenager's latest favorite star is Billie Eilish singing *No Time to Die*. It is the theme song for the new James Bond movie whose release was delayed due to the devastating COVID-19 virus that was spreading around the world.

Two lyrics in the song are:
Was I stupid to love you?
Was I reckless to help?
Was it obvious to everybody else?
That I'd fallen for a lie?
You were never on my side
Fool me once, fool me twice
Are you death or paradise?
Now you'll never see me cry
There's just no time to die

Comments on YouTube were:
"Can we talk about her talent at 18 years old please?"
"All James Bond soundtracks have a special place in my heart."
"So sad the terrible Virus moved the movie release back to November."
"Goosebumps."

Even when the teenagers agreed on the music, they found something else to disagree about.

"Move over, Sis. It's my turn to sit by the window."
"It is not," she replied. "You were there last time."
"Is to."
Is not."

After several more 'is tos' and 'is nots', our son said, "Mom, tell him it's my turn to sit by the window."

"I can't do that," I said. "I don't know whose turn it is. I have enough trouble just trying to remember where I 'm going."

Their 'automotive arguments' often started before the automobile did. "I'm going to ride in the front seat," said our older son.

"No, you aren't," said his brother. "It's my turn today."

"You're wrong," argued the older one. "You rode there last time and I had to ride in the back seat." Turning to me, he said, "Mom, tell him it's my turn."

Before I could say a word, younger son squeezed past his brother, jumped into the front seat of the car, and slammed the door behind him. Son number one pulled the outside handle to open the door and, at the same time, son number two pushed down the door lock on the inside.

Suddenly, the door was jammed into the lock position. No one could get into the front seat through the car's right-hand door, and no one could get out.

Their dear Dad had to take the broken car to a repairman who took the door apart and replaced the damaged lock mechanism. The repairman commented on how unusual it was for a door lock to become jammed. Our sons stood quietly nearby. No one revealed how the door was damaged. After that episode, they quit tampering with the door locks. They still argued about who would sit in the front seat, but they left the car door lock out of it.

It was during times like those that we needed our good sense of humor to maintain family harmony. Laughter made it easier to get through whatever automotive challenges traveled our way, when teenagers were involved. A 'joke jar' in the car often saved the day.

As Amy's daughter slid behind the wheel for her first driving lesson, she couldn't contain her excitement. "You need to make adjustments so the car is comfortable for you to drive," Amy said. "Now, what is the first thing you should do?"

"Change the radio," her daughter said.

Two teenagers were driving home one night, when one asked the other to check and see if the turning signal was working.

He promptly stuck his head out the window and said, "Yes, no, yes, no, yes, no"

You know, people don't usually compliment me on my driving," Fred said to Ted. "So, I was very pleased this morning when I saw a note on my car that said 'parking fine'. That was very nice of them."

My mother asked me to hand out invitations to my brother's surprise seventeenth birthday party. That's when I realized that he was her favorite twin.

One night about 11:00, Ron answered the phone and heard, "Dad, we want to stay out late. Is that okay?"

"Sure," Ron said. "Since you called."

When he hung up, his wife asked, "Who was that?"

"One of the boys," Ron said. "I gave them permission to stay out late."

"Not our boys," his wife said. "They're both downstairs in the basement."

A daydreaming taxi driver drove past the street his passenger lived on. The passenger leaned up from the back seat and gently tapped his driver on the shoulder.

Startled, the driver ran through a red light and almost hit a bus before he pulled over to the side of the road.

As he tried to catch his breath, the passenger said, "I'm sorry I frightened you. It's my fault."

"No, it was mine," said the driver. "This is my first day driving a cab. For the past 15 years, I drove a hearse."

Laughter draws us closer to our family. It strengthens positive feelings. We should always try to create a humor-rich environment, even in the confines of a car.

One kind word or deed can change someone's entire day.

My husband's words in the car a few years ago led me to question his kindness toward me. He was driving our car down the highway and I was sitting in the front passenger seat beside him. I noticed the red light blinking on the dashboard in front of him, indicating that my door was ajar. "Please pull over to the side of the road," I said. "My front door isn't closed."

"Just ignore that blinking light," he said. "It has a short in it. Your door isn't ajar."

I gave him a worried look out of the corner of my eye. He sounded kind and sincere about the blinking light, but had he become a dizzy driver behind the wheel, too? Was he trying to get rid of me? If my door actually flew open and I fell out along the side of the road, would he drive on and just ignore the blinking light, the drafty open door, and the empty passenger seat beside him? Was he hoping I would fall out because my driving had become a hazard to our family's health, wealth, and happiness?

Just the day before he had driven the kids to school with me in the passenger seat, against his better judgement, and our daughter had said, "Drive faster, Dad."

"I'm driving the speed limit," he replied.

"I like it better when Mom drives us to school," she said. "She gets us there faster."

Looking out the back window of the car, our son said, "Drive faster, Dad. The dog's following us."

Dad accelerated the car.

"You still aren't driving fast enough, Dad. The dog's catching up. He never catches us when Mom's driving."

Oops! Perhaps he did want to leave me along the side of the road.

No, I knew that wasn't true. We still had one more permit-driving teenager to go. My husband needed me riding in that son's passenger seat until he turned sixteen.

That son was our younger one, the one who always leaned over and honked the horn at his friends while I was driving the car. He honked the horn at pedestrians crossing in front of us. He honked the horn at cars pulling out in front of us.

I tried to keep his busy hands away from the horn, but he moved too fast for me. I had to concentrate on keeping the car on my side of the street. His honking led to moments of embarrassment for me.

If the one he honked at glared into our car, he or she naturally glared at me, the driver at the wheel of the rude and noisy horn. No one blamed my son. He was the one in the passenger seat smiling and waving at all the people.

When he turned sixteen and became the one at the wheel, I thought his honking would stop. But it didn't. It grew louder. He and his dad put an air-horn on his used car. Every day, after school or practice, I could monitor his progress from the moment he left the school's parking lot two miles away until he arrived safely home. He honked his horn all along the route.

He honked as he passed his friends in the car, or on the sidewalk, and at their homes.

He honked as he passed his grandparents' house, and he honked as he drove into our drive. He loved to honk his horn.

One day, his older brother borrowed his car to run an errand across town. When he returned, he said, "Never again. Everybody in town honked and waved at this car. It just wore me out honking and waving back at all those people I didn't know."

Teenager passengers can make a driver dizzy. Teenager drivers can make a passenger dizzy, too. Parents of teenagers get to be both, dizzy driving with them and dizzy riding with them. It takes patience for parents to survive the ordeals, patience to calmly tolerate their provocations, and patience to persevere with encouragement and kindness.

I know. I've been there. And while I was there, I prayed, "Dear God, please give me patience."

'May God, who gives this patience and encouragement, help you live in complete harmony with each other, as is fitting for followers of Christ Jesus.'
(Romans 15: 5 NLT)

"Please give me patience NOW!"

'Be still in the presence of the Lord, and wait patiently for him to act.'
(Psalms37:7a NLT)

Oops. Please forgive me my impatience. Help me to steadfastly love and endure all those enchanting times with dizzy drivers at the wheel.

Mind Your P's and Q's

Mind your P's and Q's is an old expression that may have had its beginning in the mid-19th century. There is a lot of controversy surrounding what the phrase meant then, but today it means be on your best behavior. Watch what you're saying. Watch what you're doing. Be courteous. Mind your language. Mind your manners. Practice proper etiquette.

What is etiquette?

Etiquette is a set of guidelines that controls the considerate ways a responsible individual should behave in society. It shows respect for yourself and everyone else on earth. Some people believe that these rules of good manners are outdated and unnecessary. Others contend that our good behavior toward others distinguishes us from animals. Good manners, kindness, and respect go hand in hand.

When you politely say "excuse me" and "May I", "thank you" or "I'm sorry", and "will you please ---" all in a cheerful, friendly tone of voice, you are being courteous and showing good manners.

Children are not born with the proper etiquette for interaction in society. They learn, or fail to learn, by watching and listening to the adults in their lives. Young children will quickly learn good manners when adults simply remember to treat them with courtesy and kindness and encourage them to think of others first.

Courtesy is kindness and respect in action, and kindness and respect are becoming at any age. It is a way of living that can reduce the friction and stress in human relationships.

A few more examples of good Etiquette are:

Smile.
Hold the door for the person behind you.
Look at the person speaking to you.
Be on time.

Don't initiate real personal questions about money, religion or politics.
Cough or sneeze into your elbow.
Always RSVP, and do it right away.
Shake hands firmly.
Wait until everyone is served before you start eating.
Chew silently, with your mouth closed.
Learn to say you're sorry.

His good etiquette was missing when Max pushed his way to the front of the line to get on the train. An older gentleman leaned over to Max's ear and said, "You lost something back there."
Max stepped out of line, went back along the platform and looked around but he didn't find anything.
"Keep looking," called out the older gentleman as the train left the station. "You lost your manners."

What did the older turkey say to the young turkeys on Thanksgiving?
"Mind your manners! If your Dad could see you now, he'd turn over in his gravy."

Do not let the dog sit at the table during dinner, no matter how good his manners are.

A few examples of bad etiquette are:
Talking too loud.
Staring at someone too long.
Interrupting.
Elbows on table.
Dropping trash.
Spitting, picking nose or scratching private areas.

'Love one another as brothers and sisters, and be kind and humble with one another. Do not pay back evil with evil or cursing with cursing; pay back with a blessing, because a blessing is what God promised to give you when he called you.'

(1 Peter 3:8-9 GNB)

To help all of us stay in the habit of politely thinking of others first and paying back with a blessing, we could make a point to be courteous to the first three people we meet each morning by giving sincere compliments, paying attention to their response, and not talking too much about ourselves

Dirt and grease under the fingernails are an etiquette no-no, as they tend to detract from a woman's jewelry and alter the taste of finger foods.

When watching a movie in the theatre, refrain from talking to characters on the screen. Studies have shown that they cannot hear you.

Always offer to bait your date's hook, even on the first date.

A center piece for the dinner table should never be anything prepared by a taxidermist.

What is Netiquette?
Netiquette is a set of guidelines that controls the considerate ways we should behave when using the cell phone or internet to show respect for ourselves and others. In these cyberspace times, it seems some people believe that polite rules of good manners on the internet are outdated and unnecessary.

A few examples of good netiquette are:

Remember that the person you are e-mailing or posting is a person with feelings.

Don't yell into your cell phone.

Keep personal conversations and disagreements off social networking sights.

Adhere to the same polite behavior on line that you should follow in real life.

Turn off your phone at the table.

Don't feel that you have to answer a text immediately.

Think about other people's feelings first.

Know what and who you are texting.

My friend Julie texted: "Hi, son, what does IDK, LY & TTYL mean?

He texted back: "Hi, Mom. I Don't Know, Love You & Talk To You Later."

And Julie texted him back: "It's okay, don't worry about it. I'll ask your sister. Love you, too."

Mom texting daughter Allison: Your great aunt just passed away. LOL.

Allison texting Mom: Why is that funny?

Mom: It's not funny. What do you mean?

Allison: Mom, LOL means laughing out loud.

Mom: Oh, no! I sent that text to everyone. I thought it meant lots of love. I have to call them and explain. Oh, my goodness!

After a trying day at high school, Halie settled down in her seat on the bus and closed her eyes. As the bus rolled along, the teenage lad sitting next to her pulled out his cell phone and started talking in a loud voice; "Hi, Babe. It's Alex. I'm on the bus."

"No, I'm not mad at you. I just didn't get out of class in time to see you before the bus left."

"Yes, I'm telling you the truth. Cross my heart."

Ten minutes later, he's still talking in a loud voice.

When Halie had had enough, she leaned over and said into the phone, "Honey, hang up and give me another kiss."

Alex doesn't use his phone on the bus anymore.

A panda bear walks into a restaurant. He orders a meal and eats it.

After politely paying for his meal, he pulls out a gun and shoots it in the air. Then he immediately starts toward the door.

"Why did you do that?" asked a man at the next table.

Looking back over his shoulder, the panda said, "I'm a panda. Look it up on your cell phone."

The man looked for panda bear in the dictionary on his cell phone. Finding it, he read, "Panda bear- a large black and white bear-like mammal native to the Far East. Eats shoots and leaves."

What do you do with crude oil?
Teach it manners.

A hippo wanted to join the local hippo gang. He spoke with the gang leader and was told that in order to join he had to have respect for his brothers and impeccable manners.

He nodded his head, and told the leader he was raised in a noble family with excellent etiquette. Respect and manners would come easy for him.

The hippo strutted out of the leader's room, holding his head high, proud to be part of the gang. He greeted the gangsters outside, saying "Hello' my brothers."

The gangsters laughed at him and called him nasty names.

"Darn hippo-crites!" the sad hippo said as he walked away.

Ziggy failed her driver's test today.

The instructor asked her, "What do you do at a red light?"

And she said, "I usually check my emails, my texts, and see what people are up to on Facebook."

If we unfortunately get into an argument, we should try to stick to the issue, and not bring up any past grievances. No name calling. No hitting. And no hesitating to apologize if you are wrong.

Remember to smile and gently 'kill them with kindness'. They won't know what hit them.

If we are not being polite, we are probably being rude!

Rudeness seems to be a real problem today because we, as a society, have let it take the place of common courtesy. It's no longer fashionable to smile and say 'thank you' or 'excuse me, please', but it's okay to be rude, crude, and downright disrespectful.

Being disrespectful may give immediate satisfaction, but it has long-term negative consequences. When good manners, courtesy and respect for others are not enforced, they cease to be. When our own desires for courteous consideration are not sustained, our self-respect fades away

For good manners to prevail, we need to recognize and rebuke unacceptable behavior. We can show our disapproval by avoiding the use of put-downs and abusive language. We can be a courteous example by focusing on the despicable behavior, and not on the person or his questionable ancestry.

We won't be able to change bad manners in others overnight. It will take time, just as it has taken time for us to become the rude society we are today, but good manners will cease to exist altogether if we don't change things right away.

We can start by using kindness and respect when we:

Speak –The tone and cadence of our voices affects those who hear us. A slow monotonous voice makes others think we are bored and not interested in them. Words spoken in a slightly faster cadence with enthusiasm makes others respond to us favorably.

Think – Much of what we think inside is often reflected on our faces. If we are thinking gloomy and angry thoughts, we will probably be frowning. If we feel kind and courteous toward others, we will probably be smiling. So, let's think 'smile' and put a smile on for a while. Then we can see how many smiles we will get in return.

Look – Our eyes are powerfully expressive. Even when we control our voices and wear smiles, our eyes may convey feelings of condemnation and rage. So, let's make eye contact and let others know that we respect them. Looking away or avoiding eye contact all together sends a message that we feel angry, impatient, or bored.

Laugh – Nothing works faster to bring our bodies and minds back into balance than Laughter. Humor lightens our burdens, connects us to others, inspires hope, and keeps us grounded. It also helps us release anger and forgive others sooner.

The best way to have a well-mannered teenager is to be a fine example from the moment they are born. Children watch their parents to learn what's important. They need to see that being nice to grandparents, neighbors, and people in the work force is very important.

They need to feel the love. Love is the ultimate answer.

What the World Needs Now is Love tells it all. The lyrics of this inspiring song were written by Hal David and first performed by Jackie DeShannon in 1965.
The word in the chorus are:
What the world needs now is love, sweet love
It's the only thing that there's too little of
What the world needs now is love, sweet love.
No not just for some but for everyone.

Deep down inside us we all yearn for a little kindness and respect. We all yearn for love. We will not flourish in a rude, crude, and selfish society.

So, let's make it 'cool' to say "excuse me", "please", "may I", "thank you", and you're welcome".

Let's make it 'cool' to be polite and live by the golden rule.

Is There A Doctor In The House?

Is there a doctor in the house? We need a prescription to fight criticism. Criticism is contagious. It's a communicable 'disease' that feeds on infectious germs of jealousy, envy, and ignorance.

Contagious criticism can quickly become a chronic illness if we too often criticize blindly without making an effort to become informed. Once spoken, critical words directed at others cannot be erased. Rather than heed our words and try to improve, the hearers will resent our criticism and spread the 'disease'.

Teenagers are especially vulnerable. Being a teenager isn't easy. They have a passion for living.

They are experiencing so many things in life for the first time, and they naturally start breaking away from their parents, searching for their own identity. Young people come to understand that they are members of an international age group –teenagers among teenagers – who are looking for the meaning of life. They are trying to find where they fit in.

When a teenager seems unhappy, parents would welcome a doctor in the house to guide them through their teenager's blues brought on by bitter words of contagious, destructive criticism.

But since that usually isn't going to happen, we can start helping our teenager by quietly looking to the friends he or she chooses to hang around with.

Do the friends seem unhappy? Are they belligerent and angry at the world? Do they blame everyone else for their problems? Do they fail to get along with THEIR parents?

If the answer to all four questions is "yes", that's the bad news. But, the worst news is the more sensitive and empathetic your teenager is by nature – in short, the 'nicer' he or she is – the more likely he or she will become the victim of another teenager's negative, critical, and jealous words.

The experience of being criticized by their peers and fake friends saps an adolescent of self-esteem. It's important to recognize how our teenager may be affected by others. Encourage conversations. Be ready to listen at any time, any place.

So, how did we help our teenager make good friends? We started by suggesting he or she watch a kind person who seemed to have a lot of good friends. What did people like about that person? Was he or she smiling? Was she funny and entertaining? Was he kind? Did she maintain eye contact and listen quietly when someone else was talking?

Then we encouraged our teenager to follow these good examples:

Give sincere compliments with a smile.

Pay attention. Look eye to eye. Listen. Don't interrupt.

Don't talk too much about yourself. That makes you a boring person.

To get a teenage friend talking, try asking some of these questions:

Who is your favorite hero, and why?

If you could be an animal, what would you be, and why?

If you could go anywhere in the world where would you go, and why?

I was reprimanding our teenage son for not getting his Advanced Algebra homework turned in on time --- again! And I reminded him that driving his car to school was a privilege not a requirement.

117

He quietly listened, then gently smiled and said, "Thank you, Mom. I'll try harder. I know I'll appreciate this when I'm older."

What? Good one, son, I thought. You know the consequences. Doing homework equals car. Not doing homework equals no car. Good choice of kind words. The choice is yours.

Point taken. So, I gently smiled back and said, "You're welcome."

We need to learn to not be so hard on others or ourselves. We need to learn to share the laughter.

Ben's Mom said, "You weren't even listening, were you?"

And Ben thought, "That's a weird way to start a conversation."

"Why are pediatricians always angry?
"Because they have little patients."

"Doctor", Quincy said. "I keep seeing an insect buzzing around me."

"Don't worry," his doctor replied. "That's just a bug going around."

Ron said, "If cold, you should go stand in a corner."
"Why," asked Lon.
"Because it is 90 degrees there."

In the Wild West a long time ago, a young man named Chet was riding shotgun on top with the stagecoach driver. He looked into the distance and said to the driver, "Hank, I see a little bitty thing on the horizon. I think it's an indian.

"Well, shoot him," Hank replied.

"I can't," said Chet. "He's too far away."

A short while later, Chet said, "He's getting closer."

"Can you shoot him now?" Asked the driver.

"No, but he's gaining on us!" A few minutes later, Chet said, "He's at the back of the stagecoach."

"Shoot him now!" Hank shouted. "Shoot him now!"

Chet lowered his rifle, shook his head and said, "I can't. I've known him since he was a little bitty thing."

It's our responsibility to help a teenager understand that to have a friend, we must first be a friend, even to ourselves. A real friend is someone who will stand by us in rough times as well as smooth times. A real friend is loyal, helpful and dependable. A real friend can keep a secret. Real friends can disagree without feeling threatened. A real friend is not jealous.

Beware of jealousy. Jealousy can ruin a friendship. When someone is jealous, everyone involved is a victim, including the jealous one. Everyone gets hurt. Jealousy can make people feel angry and bitter. It can ruin the relationship. Those involved may become obsessed with getting even. They can't think straight. Emotions take over.

They start criticizing to anyone who will listen. Many people thrive on criticism, gossip, and out-right lies. They can't wait to pass it on, and the critical words become a vicious virus spreading like wildfire.

Critical words, once said, cannot be detracted. They burn into the receiver's mind and fester there.

So, how do we handle criticism and what do we say to our troubled teenagers?

1-Beware of people who come up to you and say, "I hate to tell you this but it's for your own good." Very likely it isn't for your own good, but for their jealous feelings toward your 'good'.

2-Don't let yourself be bothered by what people say as long as you know deep down what is right for you.

3-Don't waste time saying, "it's not my fault" and criticizing others if the fault happens to lie with you.

4-Don't ignore ALL criticism directed at you.
Learn to recognize the unjust, and listen to the just.
Criticism given constructively helps you grow as you go.

'Get rid of all bitterness rage, anger, harsh words, and slander, as well as all types of evil behavior. Instead, be kind to each other, tenderhearted, forgiving one another.'

(Ephesians 4:31 NLT)

The more respectful and considerate we are, the more people envy us and want to criticize us, so let us accept unfounded criticism as a compliment in disguise.

In his book, *How to Stop Worrying and Start Living*, Dale Carnegie stated: "Any fool can criticize, condemn and complain --- and most fools do. But it takes character and self-control to be understanding and forgiving".

Choose words wisely. Words are free. It's how we use them that may cost us.

We can choose to use them with kindness and respect as we convey words of encouragement and praise, or we can choose to use them with destructive criticism by wielding words of despair.

The words we speak or write to our family and others carry a powerful punch and create a lasting memory. Our words can make or break a relationship, and the way we express ourselves can improve or destroy our family ties.

What is said to a child shapes his or her experiences and beliefs. Through the teenager years and on into adulthood, the individual talks to himself, or herself, and others the way he or she was spoken to during the young, formative years. That is how we shape the world.

Words have power. What we say to ourselves and others makes all the difference in our lives, our self-esteem, and the future. Be diligent. Be mindful before we speak. Concentrate on powerful words and responses. Know the different emotions words can convey.

Negative, destructive words –never, no, careless, pitiful, weak, sneaky, menacing, awful, corrupt, ugly, disgraceful, and lazy.

Positive, constructive words – yes, proud, pleased, happy, great, good, graceful, exciting, joyful, grateful, patient, and love.

Spiritual, compassionate words – faith, hope, love, courage, confidence, and gratitude.

Destroy vulgar words.

As parents, we should walk the walk and talk the talk by trying to speak calmly, in a loving tone, and getting kids to listen without yelling. Remind them that their behavior has consequences. Choosing the consequences by their actions and words is their choice. Strive to be consistent.

Keep your thought positive because your thoughts become your words.
Keep your words positive because your words become your behavior.
Keep your behavior positive because your behavior becomes your habits.
Keep your habits positive because your habits become your values.
Keep your values positive because your values become your destiny.
Mahatma Gandhi

We can choose to be happy, and think before we speak. One kind word can change someone's entire day. So, if we can't say something kind, we shouldn't say anything.

Maintain a sense of humor. Find some jokes to share.

The other day my sister asked for her lipstick, but I accidently pass her a glue stick.

She still isn't speaking to me.

"What did one earthquake say to the other?"
"It's not my fault."

Jadyn went to the doctor and said, "I'm dying."

"What's wrong?" asked the doctor.
Jadyn pointed to several parts of his body and said, "It hurts here, here, , and ---".
The doctor looked at Jadyn's hand and said, "Your finger's broken."

Three brothers named Manners, Trouble and Shut Up were playing hide and seek. Shut Up was 'it'. He found Manners right away, so they both started searching for their brother.
They looked for hours and still could not find him.
Finally, they went to the police station. Manners was shy so he stayed outside, and Shut Up went in to talk to the officer.
"What's your name?" asked the officer.
"Shut Up."
"How rude! Where's your manners?"
"Waiting outside."
"Okay ---," said the officer. "What are you doing here?"
And Shut Up said, "Looking for Trouble."

A priest and a pastor from two local churches stood by the side of the road and pounded a sign into the ground. The sign said: "The End is Near! Turn Yourself Around Now – Before it is Too Late!"
A car sped by and the driver yelled, "Leave us alone, you religious nuts!"
From around the curve the priest and pastor heard screeching tires and a big splash.

The pastor turned to the priest and said, "Do you thing the sign should just say, 'Bridge Out'?

Everyone thought Roger was such a nice guy. In middle school, his teachers would always asking if he had done his homework and he would hold up his papers and say 'yes'. At lunch, classmates would always ask if they could sit with him and he would say 'yes'. A kid would ask if he would trade his banana for an apple, and he would always say, 'yes'. Everyone was amazed by how generous, nice and positive he was.

In high school, Roger was asked to join the football team. He said 'yes' and they won their conference. Some other students asked if he would tutor them and he said 'yes'.

After college, he was offered a great job and he said 'yes'. Every time he was offered a promotion he said 'yes'. When a hospital asked for a donation he said 'yes'. When the school asked him for a donation he said 'yes'.

Then Roger's girlfriend proposed and he said 'yes'. Being his oldest and closest friend, Mark was asked to be Roger's best man. "I'll do it," Mark said. "But first, tell me why you always say 'yes' to everything."

Roger simply smiled and said, "I don't no."

What did the math book say to the English book?
"I'm jealous. You are full of stories and I'm just full of problems."

Which letters are always jealous?
NV

Laughter is the best medicine. We don't need a doctor in the house if we serve a dose of kind laughter with love, and choose our words carefully.

It was April when I took a sack of garbage to the garage and tripped over one of my daughter's all-occasion tennis shoes laying at the back door. My ankle twisted, and gave way beneath me. I fell to the concrete floor, and called out to my teenage children, "Help! I twisted my ankle and I can't get up."

They came out to the garage and surrounded my fallen body, but no one offered to help me up. They just looked down at me and laughed.

"I'm hurt, and you three are laughing," I said. "That's no way to treat your only mother."

"Stop with the joke, Mom. We know what day it is. You can't fool us again. You're up to your old tricks on April Fool's Day."

They looked. They saw the swelling. And, at last, they started to believe that I might be telling the truth. All three of them helped me hobble into the house, but we had a terrible time getting me to a chair. We were all laughing so hard about their cautious reaction to my for-real fall.

"Fine bunch you are," I said, as I wiped away the tears of laughter, because I'd played so many jokes on them before, and now the joke was on me. "Remind me next time to have my accident on any day but April fool's Day."

We didn't need a doctor in the house for my slightly twisted ankle. We shared the laughter. Laughter was indeed the best medicine.

Let's all try to do the best we can to rise above this crippling "criticism disease'. Although there may not be a doctor in the house, we are never alone.

If critical words start to get us down, we can just remember a few words of this song and our internal harmony will be restored.

You'll Never Walk Alone
When you walk through a storm
 Hold your head up high
 And don't be afraid of the dark
 At the end of a storm
 There's a golden sky
 And the sweet silver song of a lark
 Walk on through the wind

Walk on through the rain
Though your dreams be tossed and blown
Walk on, walk on
With hope in your heart
And you'll never walk alone
You'll never walk alone
    The song was written by Oscar Hammerstein II and
Richard Rogers for their 1945 musical *Carousel*.
Christine Johnson first sang the song.

    May our goal be to walk on with hope in our hearts,
doing the best we can to accept any negative criticism as
a stepping stone to success. May we identify unjust
criticism as the sound of jealousy or envy, then ignore it.
    By becoming immune to unfounded criticism and
considering the feelings of others, we will help control
this 'communicably crippling disease' called criticism
that is spreading unchecked across the land.

Who Let the Ducks Out?

Animals play important roles in our lives. They depend on us, their keepers, for food, kindness, and friendship. In return, they offer unconditional love. Even ducks respect and follow the one who feeds them. When our teenagers were younger, we gave them three baby ducks at Easter time. Our kids were fascinated by their webbed feet, wide bills with air holes, and waddling walks.

They named the ducks Donald Duck, Quacker, and Little Bit. We learned how fast tiny yellow ducks grew, how much ducks ate, and how messy they were. Every few days, we had to find a larger boxes for their bed in the basement.

During the day, they played in a backyard portable pen. It was funny watching our 'Duck Master Daughter' open the garage door onto the patio and call out, "Come on, Ducks."

Then she would walk to the portable pen with the three ducks waddling close behind her, their feet slap-slap-slapping on the concrete patio in time with their quack-quack-quacking.

The ducks depended on 'Duck Master Daughter' to feed and water them. Whenever they saw her in the yard, they quacked for her attention.

Then disaster struck. Donald Duck suddenly died. No autopsy was performed, but since he was our biggest duck we diagnosed that he ate himself to death.

Feathers grew on the remaining two. In six short weeks, they changed from tiny downy yellow ducklings into big fat white-feathered ducks. Finally, we decided to move them to a pond in the country where other ducks lived. Within a week, our ducks had disappeared. We diagnosed that they had been eaten by the foxes who lived in a den down the road.

It was a sad day, when we said farewell to our ducks. We found a song to remember them by. Bryant Oden wrote *The Duck Song and the Lemonades Stand* in 2008. A few of the verses go like this:

(Bum bum bum, ba-dum ba-dum)
A duck walked up to a lemonade stand
And he said to the man, running the stand
"Hey! (bum bum bum) Got any grapes?"
The man said "No we just sell lemonade.
But it's cold
And it's fresh and it's all home-made.
Can I get you a glass?"
The duck said, "I'll pass".
(chorus)
Then he waddled away.
(waddle waddle)
'Til the very next day.
(Bum bum bum bumba-bada-dum)

There are six more stanzas that follow with the duck wanting grapes, and the chorus repeated in between. Then there's a surprise ending. It is a good learn-to-sing song on YouTube.

Our ducks were not allowed in the house because our dog did not like all their slapping, quacking and pooping. Since the dog came before the ducks, the dog ruled. Our first house dog was Spooks. He was a black miniature poodle, and he thought that everyone came to the house to see him.

He went wild with excitement, jumping up and down, licking faces and barking constantly. We tried scolding him, and he loved the attention. We chased him with a folded newspaper, and he loved the attention. We threw pillows at him, and he loved the attention.

Nothing worked. All the attention we gave him for misbehaving made him misbehave even more.

127

One day when Spooks was three, he ran out in front of a car. Our younger son saw the car coming and shouted a warning. But Spooks didn't listen. I saw the car coming and shouted a warning. But Spooks didn't listen. He ran into the street, under the wheels of the car, and died instantly because he was always too excited to listen.

After we held a small memorial service and buried Spooks in the shade of a large oak tree, Dear Dad sadly shook his head and said, "No more dogs".

"How lucky I am to have something that makes saying good-bye so hard."
Winnie the Pooh

Three months later, we got our second miniature poodle. He was chocolate-colored, and the kids named him Chocolate Chip --- Chip, for short. He was a good, obedient dog --- except for one bad habit. He wanted to escape and run all over town. But there was a leash law. Animals within the city limits had to be on a leash at all times.

One day, when Chip was two years old, he broke loose from his chain in the backyard, and he ran away. He was gone for three hours. That night, after he returned home, he became violently ill. He went into convulsions on the family room floor. I rushed him to the veterinary clinic, and they sedated him to stop the convulsing.

He died two days later. Somewhere, while he was running loose, Chip apparently drank from a puddle or bottle of antifreeze. Although antifreeze is a deadly poison, dogs love the taste of it.

After we held a small memorial service and buried Chip in the shade of the large oak tree, Dear Dad said in a sad voice, "No more dogs".

Three months later, Jingles came to live with us. Jingles was a very smart dog about a lot of things. She was more obedient than any of our children. She didn't talk back or roll her eyes, or shrug her shoulders.

She didn't blame anyone else when things went wrong, and she didn't complain when someone else was blaming her. She just wagged her tail, stuck out her tongue, and smiled.

I found a wad of gum on our younger son's bedpost. "How did that get there?" I asked.

He shrugged his shoulders and said, "It must have been the dog."

I found a wad of bubble gum under an end table in the rec room. "How did that get there?" I asked our daughter, who was a possible culprit.

She shrugged her shoulders and said, "It must have been the dog."

I found a wad of bubble gum beneath a kitchen chair. "How did that get there?" I asked our older son who had been sitting in the chair.

He shrugged his shoulders and said, "It must have been the dog."

"That does it," I said. "No more bubble gum in the house until Jungles learns to throw it into the garbage when she's through with it. We have to teach her a lesson."

Our three guilty teenagers ducked their 'tails' and ran.

We didn't know how smart Jingles really was until the morning we were going to go away for a few days and leave her behind at the veterinary clinic, as we had done several times before. Our son said, "I hate to admit it, but it's my turn to take Jingles to the v-e-t." (He spelled the word instead of saying it.)

Upon hearing the letters v-e-t, Jingles ran for the sofa, crawled under it, and hid. She could spell! We knew she understood the word vet, but, until that moment, we didn't know that she could spell it as well.

When we left the house for a few hours during the day, we put Jingles in the half-bath off the kitchen so she wouldn't get into mischief while we were gone. As we got ready to leave, she wagged her tail and smiled, hoping that the outing included her.

Then, as soon as she heard someone say, "Put Jingles in the bathroom", she ran under the sofa to hide.

So, we started spelling in front of her again. And, in a few days, as soon as she heard the letters b-a-t-h-r-o-o-m, she ran under the sofa to hide.

Someone suggested we use sign language. But we didn't try it. We figured that, as smart as Jingles was, she would memorize the sign language faster than any of us.

Jingles lived in our house for thirteen years. Then, one day as her health was failing, she tried to crawl under the sofa and broke her back. Her pain was horrible. Our grief was intense. Our older son took her to the vet one last time and sadly said "Good-bye".

At the end of that fatal day, our younger son came home from an after-school event and complained to his brother, "You took Jingles away before I had a chance to say good-bye!"

Our older son felt awful. "Why is he blaming me, Mom?" He asked.

"Don't worry," I said. "Your brother is just having trouble facing the terrible reality of death."

"But he was here before I took Jingles to the vet. He saw how bad she was. He heard you say that she was going to sleep, and we wouldn't see her again."

"I know," I said, hugging my son. "He chose to avoid the awful truth that his dog was going to die. And now that he's so upset and angry about losing his dog, he's trying to blame everyone but himself for not spending more time with her before she died. We all have to learn how to accept death in our lives. It's very difficult."

Although it was difficult to accept the loss of pets they had loved, our children learned that, as time passed, the intense grief faded. And later, even with new pets in their lives, they always had fond memories in their hearts of those they had lost.

"If there ever comes a day when we can't be together, keep me in your heart, I'll stay there forever." Winnie the Pooh

In addition to the ducks and dogs, we had a cross-eyed Siamese cat named Clarence, a black and white cat named Mystic Seaport, and a striped cat named Thunder Hole (places we had visited during our family trip along the New England Seacoast). Our one and only parakeet was named Ranger because he came from Texas. We had hamsters (with names I can't remember), and a guinea pig named Lightning. We also had unnamed tropical fish several years ago until I caught our younger son drinking out of the aquarium.

Naming our pets involved major family conferences, and long discussions, with lots of laughter to save the sanity. Some dog-name suggestions were Brunhilda, Chewbarka, and Sherlock Bones.

"If we had three dogs, we could name them Peanut, Butter and Jelly." (That wasn't going to happen.)

"Let's name the dog Damn-it. Then if we're mad at him, we can say, 'Damn-it dog'."

"If we had a chicken, we could name it Repecka." (No way!)

"We could name our cats Lucifurr, Jennyanydots, or Toast."

"Toast is a good name. Then if the cat walks on Dad's car, he can say, "Your Toast!"

Brandon named his dog 5-miles. Now he can tell people he walks 5-miles every day.

"What do you feed a dog with fever?"
"Mustard. It works well with a hot dog."

Zeke has two watch dogs.
Their names are Rolex and Timex.

Annalise's dog ripped the blanket off her last night.
But she will recover.

Where do dogs go when their tails fall off?
The re-tail store.

Where do you take someone who has been injured
in a Peek-a-boo accident?
To the I.C.U.

When we found uninvited animals in our house, our
teenagers laughed a lot. First, there were mice. Some
people may say 'mice are nice', but you will not hear
those words from me. If a pesky mouse got into our
house, it always waited to jump out at me. Not my
husband, or our teenagers. Just me.

If a mouse jumped out at me, I screamed, and our
teenagers came running. Of course, they didn't come to
rescue me, or to help catch the mouse. They came to
watch their mother shake and shiver because she was
afraid of the "cute' little thing.

They came to point and laugh at the sight of me
standing on the nearest table or countertop, or chair.

One morning, I met a mouse in the bathroom, and it
wasn't even his turn to be there. My husband had gone
in first. Did the mouse jump out at him? No,

It waited until I went in, and then: Surprise!
Surprise!

I forgot why I was there, and ran out screaming, "A
mouse! There's a great big mouse in the house!"

My brave husband, who was barely dressed, picked
up his nearest shoe, marched into the bathroom, and
closed the door. I huddled in the hall waiting for the
final results.

Behind the door came loud sounds of beating,
banging, and falling about.

Suddenly, all was quiet
Who had won? Man or mouse?
Slowly, the door creaked open.

Out came my brave husband with a mouse by the tail.

But I wondered, was it really the same mouse? It looked so small, hanging there in the air at the end of its tail.

One evening as I opened the dishwasher, a mouse jumped out at me, and I screamed!

On another day as I opened the kitchen towel drawer, a mouse jumped out at me, and I screamed!

On a dark and stormy night I opened a closet door for the ironing board, a mouse jumped out at me, and I screamed!

When the mice jumped and I screamed, I knew my fears were unfounded. I knew I was bigger than they were. But when I found mice in the house, all those logical thoughts went 'out the window'.

I sincerely wished those pesky mice would jump out at the teenagers in our house once in a while instead of me, always me. But come to think of it, they would probably love the surprise, name all the mice, and beg to keep them as pets.

When our two sons and a neighborhood friend moved the woodpile in our backyard, they found a nest of baby mice that were no longer skinless pink but slightly covered in grey fur. Not knowing what they were up to, I innocently stepped outside at precisely the wrong moment. Our older son picked up a tiny mouse and chased me around the house. His friend met me in front of the house with another mouse, and he chased me across the yard.

I ran inside, and slumped into a chair at the kitchen table to pamper my pounding heart. Our younger son came into the house. "Are you all right, Mom?" He asked in a concerned voice.

I nodded 'yes' cautiously, very cautiously. I appreciated his concern, but I was a little surprised that he wasn't chasing me with a mouse, too. He was the biggest tease of all.

Reaching out, he gently laid his hand on my wrist. I looked down.

A skinny grey tail was lying on the back of his hand, protruding out from beneath the cuff of his long-sleeve shirt. He had a mouse up his sleeve!

I screamed, jumped up, and ran away from my laughing teenager son.

I should have known not to trust his concern. He was always carrying new 'pets 'into the house and 'accidentally' letting them loose. We've chased his frogs through the living room, looked for his caterpillars under the bed, and found his toads in the toilet.

One day, as I was writing on my computer while the kids were away at school, I felt something land on top of my head.

Then it began to crawl in my hair.

I grabbed --- and caught a giant grasshopper in my hand. I didn't know how it got into the house, but I expected to find an empty jar somewhere, a jar that once held a giant grasshopper, and belonged to our younger son, the creature-collector.

Several years ago, I found cockroaches in the house. No one knew how they got in. Even our young creature-collector didn't do THAT. I spotted a cockroach on the basement wall, then I saw two more in one of the kitchen cabinets. I was mortified! We had to get rid of them. Immediately!

That evening when my husband came home from the bank, work-weary and worn-out, I met him at the door with three roaches sealed in an air-tight jelly jar. "See these," I said. "You have to do something about them. Now!"

He wasn't as upset about the bugs as I was. He was tired. "They're roaches, all right," he said, and sat down in his favorite chair to rest. He spent the evening there, as I ran through the house looking for roaches everywhere.

That night I dreamed bugs were crawling all over my body. And I imagined I could hear them scurrying up the walls in the dark. The house had to be sprayed for bugs as soon as possible!

At breakfast the next morning, I set a box of Raisin Bran in front of my dear husband who wasn't worrying about the roaches. He filled his cereal bowl with cereal, then added milk and sugar.

As he raised a spoonful to his mouth, I said, "I hope all the black things in your cereal are raisins, and not roaches."

He put down his spoon, picked up the phone, and called a speedy exterminator. For some reason, he didn't finish his bowl of cereal that morning, and he hasn't wanted Raisin Bran since.

When it came to animal traumas in the house, we tried to look to the funny side by stepping back and searching for the humor in the situations. Instead of getting up tight and not letting it go, we tried to take it lightly, and share the laughter --- after the exterminator left.

Some people say, "If you don't have a sense of humor, you don't have any sense at all."

Losing our precious pets was a different story altogether, but we still needed to maintain our sense of humor and cherish the memories with one another. Pets can teach their family a lot about life and death.

Our kids learned to be responsible as they provided food, shelter and kindness for their pets. And they learned about grieving after the loss of a precious pet. It was a sad time for them. Death is always sad.

Although it's difficult to accept the loss of a pet we have loved, we have learned that, as time passes, the deep sorrow fades. And later, even with new pets in our lives, we will always carry fond memories of those we have lost.

The sudden death of a pet reminds us that life is too short to waste a moment worrying about those 'pet peeves' that really BUG us.

Those we love don't go away. They walk beside us every day, unseen, unheard, but always near and always dear.

Family Values, Laughter, Values Family

Family values give meaning and direction to every part of family life. Values are a family's belief about what is important and what is not. Each family has their own personal set of values. Those values are all the things we treasure, a code of conduct, an appreciation of wisdom and material possessions, and an understanding of right and wrong.

The first rule for instilling family values is to live by the rules. Be a good example. Give back that extra dollar the sales clerk handed you by mistake. Don't throw that trash out the car window. Apologize for hurting your daughter's feelings.

If we want to make a connection with teenagers, we should sit down with them and ask them what their most important family values are.

Start with **code of conduct**. These values included kindness, respect, honesty, cleanliness, health, happiness, and humor. That's the beginning of my list. Now, what is yours?

We had a code of conduct during board games and card games at our house. No name calling. No hitting. No pounding on the table. No bending the rules. No exceptions.

At the end of the game, the winners said, "Good game" and the losers said, "Congratulations".

Sometimes, the looks on the loser's faces made others laugh. So, they quickly had to remember it was just a game, and learn to laugh at themselves first.

It seemed that I always had to remember to laugh at myself first. One Saturday afternoon, I carried a box of books to the basement to store it on top of a tall stack of freestanding metal shelves that held numerous boxes of other 'valuable' items. I lifted the box of books up to the top shelf and unconsciously used the bottom self of the unit for leverage.

Suddenly, the shelf tower and all its contents came tumbling down on top of me. Boxes fell all around me. Stuff spilled over me. The loud sounds of crashing and breaking could be heard throughout the house.

I groaned beneath the weight of everything on top of me.

Then, off in the distance, I heard one of my teenage children laughing. "Did you hear that awful noise?"

"Yeah," said another. "It sounds like Mom's up to one of her tricks again."

"Should we go check on her?"

"I suppose, but she'd better not yell 'April Fool'. That was six months ago."

They found me beneath the rubble, realized it was no joke, and hurried to help me escape from the mess.

After they learned that I wasn't hurt, we laughed and laughed over how unsympathetic they were to their poor, old mother. I knew I deserved their hesitation in coming to my rescue. I had teased them many times before.

Our teenage sons had a lot of fun teasing their one and only sister, too. One teasing subject was cemeteries. Yes, cemeteries.

When we were on a vacation in Mississippi, she pointed to three tall crosses set high on a hill in a huge cemetery on the side of the highway, and said, "What a lovely cemetery!"

Forever after, when her brothers saw a field of tombstones, they turned to her and said in unison, "Oh, look, Sis. A lovely cemetery! Your favorite thing."

There were many cemeteries pointed out to her on our journeys. Too many. And yet, if one of her brothers happened to miss one along the way, her dad and I found ourselves joining in the teasing fun, pointing out the lovely cemeteries as we rode along.

We were riding along a highway in Tennessee, when our older son saw a fallen wooden barricade with brown sandbags to secure it in place. The barricade was laying at the side of the road. "Oh," he said in a sad voice. "A dead deer."

Then he got a closer look and realized his mistake. "It's just a fallen barricade," he said.

Everyone in the car had heard him say 'a dead deer' and, from that day to this, when any of us in the family see a barricade along the side of the road, we say, "Don't look, brother! It's a barricade. We don't want you to get upset."

Just the other day, my darling daughter said, "Remember that time in the desert when Mom thought the humidity gauge in our motorhome was stuck on zero, and she hurt her hand pounding on it, until we convinced her that there was no humidity in the hot, dry desert?"

139

Everyone remembered and laughed. So did I, because if I can't take their teasing, I can't tease them about the funny moments in their past.

All in the family teasing may vary from one family to another, but our bodies are healthier, our hearts are happier, and we have a lot more fun when we learn to loosen up and laugh at all the silly things we do.

Our **code of wisdom** encompassed family values on words, common sense, education, cooperation, money matters, work ethics, and humor.

To help us choose words wisely, our family valued the fascinating realm of words. We often displayed a new word for the day on the front of our refrigerator and discussed it at the dinner table.

Okay. The word for the day was palindrome. Do you know what it means? Here's a hint. The title of this chapter *Family Values, Laughter, Values Family* is a palindrome. Why?

It reads the same forward and backwards.

We had some fun with it. We asked the family to create palindromes of their own. Some of their creations were:

"Madam, I'm Adam."
"Red rum, sir, is murder."
"No lemon, no melon."
"Was it a cat I saw?"
"Do geese see God?"

Palindromes are found in modern and classical music, and they are found in numbers (191, 313, and 757). They are also found is words. Some palindromic words are:

Kayak
Hannah
Racecar
Solos
Level

Make it a game. See how many the family can name.

Semordnilap (palindromes spelled backwards) is a name for words that spell different words in reverse. Two examples of this are; Alucard (Dracula spelled backwards) and stressed (desserts spelled backwards).

According to the Reader's Digest, the following are some of the most beautiful words in the English language:

Sibilance – beautiful because of the hiss-like s sounds

Loquacious – beautiful with the qu sound and a kind way to say someone talks a lot

Epiphany – beautiful because of the ph sound and a bright idea

Serendipity – just plain fun to say a word meaning good fortune

My beautiful word choice is phenomenon. It makes me happy. I want to sing with the Muppets every time I hear the word.

We had fun with word-mystery messages. An example is below.

STAND	TAKING	2	TAKING
I	UR	THROW	MY

(Answer: I understand UR undertaking 2 overthrow my undertaking.)

"What starts with E, ends with E, and has one letter in the middle?"
"Envelope."

"Thanks for explaining 'many' to me. It means a lot."

Some people think prison is one word ... but to robbers it's a whole sentence.

Family values and the matter of money continued to be an ongoing discussion. Money is simply a matter of mind over matter. If you don't mind, money doesn't matter.

There was nothing wrong or unhealthy about our teenagers wanting a reasonable amount of material goods to a reasonable degree, and within the lines of what we could afford. All teenagers want things. It's only natural. Just a half-hour of television can transform a once happy teenager into a discontented shopper because he or she doesn't have the right hoodie, sexy cologne, or all-occasion tennis shoes.

Our family agreed on three factors regarding money matters.

1-Set a clothing, electronics, and supplies budget.
2-Save for those special purchases.
3-It's good to want something and not get it. That builds character.

If our teenagers asked for certain items that were out of our financial reach. We didn't hesitate to tell them the truth. They were more understanding about what we could and could not afford when we took the time to explain our living expenses to them, instead of just saying "no". No one's self-esteem was damaged in any way.

Even with the amenable money matters discussions, we had a lot of "I need" requests.

"Hey, Mom and Dad, I need a car." (Says who?)
"I need $68 for a high school class ring."
"I need $40 for art supplies."
"I need a car." (Says who?)"
"I need $55 for a pair of track shoes."
"I need a new jacket."
"But you already have three jackets. Where are they?"
"I left them at school and its cold outside this morning."
"I need a new bottle of glue."
"Where's the glue I bought you last week?"

142

"All over Tommy's shirt, but he squirted first."

"I need a car." (Says who?)

Our **code of spiritual values** included prayer, worship, humor, gratitude, faith, hope, and love.

Through a ritual of daily prayers at the table before we ate, it was my hope that our family would grow together in faith, hope, and love, and that they would stay away from the trap of God on Sunday and 'me' the rest of the week. We all took turns offering the mealtime prayers. When the children were younger, they would argue, "It's *my* turn to say the prayer."

"No, it's *my* turn to say it. You prayed last time."

"You're both wrong," insisted child number three. "It's *my* turn."

Their dad put an end to the arguing by randomly choosing who would say the prayer.

We had to listen carefully because we never knew what to expect. One Thursday when we sat down to eat, dear old Dad said to our younger son, "Please say the prayer for us."

And our son began to pray, "Dear God, watch me safely through the night … "

"Hold it," interrupted his dad. "Son, are you eating or sleeping?"

"Eating."

"Then save that prayer for later," his dad said with a smile. "Please say an eating prayer before we all fall asleep at the table."

As our kids became teenagers, we asked them to create their own prayers. One day, when it was our daughter's turn, she offered a beautiful prayer thanking God for family, friends, and animals, then thanking Him for our food, and asking Him to bless the hands that prepared it as well as bless it to the nourishment of our bodies. As she said, "Amen," both boys grabbed for the food in front of them.

"Hey, what's going on here?" I asked.

143

"Her prayer was too long. I almost starved to death," said one brother.

"Yeah," said the other. "And the french fries are getting cold. She may have eaten snacks after school, but I didn't."

A few days later, when our daughter finished praying again, the boys started to grab as before. "Stop," ordered their dad. "From now on when we say prayers, I want everyone's head bowed, all eyes closed, and hands still. That's the way to pray. No one should have his hand on the meat platter or his eye on the applesauce. Is that clear, boys?"

"Yes, Dad," they said in unison.

Then in a small voice, one of them said, "But how did you know we were doing those things if you had your head bowed and your eyes closed during the prayer?"

And we all had to laugh, for we knew it didn't hurt to pray with humor in our hearts. If God didn't have humor in His heart, He would have given up on us a long, long time ago.

Talking to God in prayer about our problems brings us peace because, no matter how young or old we are, when we give our worries to God, we've done our very best.

We should have as much faith in prayer as these two children did.

Little Timmy was riding on a long trip in a hot car, and he said, "Mommy, I need rain!"

She flippantly said, "Ask Jesus."

Timmy pointed all around and said, "Jesus, please give me rain."

Five minutes later, raindrops fell on the car.

Young Nora caught her finger in the car door. Later in the day, her mother overheard her praying, "Jesus, please make my finger okay, but wait until after my daddy comes home and sees it."

Worshipping together with our church family was an important spiritual value. When our children became teenagers, their dad and I taught the High School Class and took on the role of youth group leaders in our church. We held that position for seven years and chaperoned many social gatherings for the youth of our church. Every last one of those teenagers were Kind, respectful, and fun.

They didn't give us any terrible trauma we couldn't handle. We had a wonderful time, as long as we anticipated their next surprise move, and tried to stay one step ahead of them.

We vowed to be positive-minded leaders. Positive people attract teenagers, while negative people repel them. We listened. We sympathized. And we smiled. Smiles not only made us feel good, but it made everyone around us feel good, too.

I was smiling as I drove eight happy teenagers to a church outing in our family van. When the traffic light ahead of me turned red, I came to a safe stop.

Suddenly, the unexpected happened. The teenagers riding with me opened all the doors. They jumped out, ran around the van in the midst of stopped traffic, and hopped in the van again, using different doors and taking different seats.

"What was that?" I asked in a surprised voice.

"Chinese fire drill!" They all shouted, and laughed.

I smiled. "Okay, but no more, please," I said. "One unexpected Chinese fire drill   an evening is all the excitement my poor heart can stand."

They all laughed at my surprised reaction. I laughed, too. Then they respected my wishes and did not do another drill that evening.

Later, as we were returning home that same evening, I stopped at another red light. A semi-trailer truck stopped in the right hand lane beside me. The teenage girl in our front passenger seat rolled down her window. "Hi," she said to the young truck driver. "You're cute. Want to ride with us?"

"Sure," he said. "Why not?"

We drove on, with everyone in the van laughing, just as the teenage girl next to me had hoped we would do.

Although I was laughing, too, I watched the truck in my rearview mirror. Before the next stop light, I changed lanes to the right hand side of the intersection, putting the truck behind me.

"Why did you do that?" asked the teenage girl beside me. "I wanted to talk to the truck driver again."

"I thought so," I said with a smiled. "That's why I'm not taking any chances. I don't want you to talk him into following us home."

We grinned at each other. Then, suddenly, she sobered and whispered, "Don't tell my mom."

I laughed and whispered back, "I won't."

What was there to tell? Nothing had happened. She had been having a little fun. No harm was done. The truck driver didn't follow us home. I saw to that. And when I suggested she stop, she did. It was simply another example of handling the unexpected that I had learned to expect when I was with teenagers on a church outing.

My husband and I served a 'mixed-up dinner' to 20 teenagers in our basement recreation room and, all evening long, the laughter rang out loud and clear.

We held Christmas gatherings and birthday parties in our basement for the teenagers from church and encouraged them to invite their friends. Then, before we knew it, a lot of their friends stated attending our church, too.

The teenagers enjoyed playing the game of Charades. My husband was the official time-keeper for the games, and I was the 'honesty' judge. Everyone there had good, clean fun, acting out song or movie titles for their teammates to guess in record time.

There was never a hint of illegal teenage drinking at any of the church parties we held for the teenagers and their invited friends. We had no problems with beer being smuggled in. And we didn't have to warn them. They already knew that we didn't have to drink to have a good time at our parties, so they respected our examples, and didn't have to drink at theirs.

During our Saturday-night lock-ins at the church for the teenagers and their friends, we had two simple, but firm rules.

No one comes in or goes out of the church after all doors are locked at 7:00 p.m. on Saturday.

No one goes home until after they have attended church with the group on Sunday morning.

We trusted the teenagers to follow the rules. And they did. Every single time. Sixty-five teenagers stayed all night at the church on Saturday nights. They ate pizza, popcorn, and snacks galore. They sang songs, watched movies, and played games all night long. Then sixty-five sleepy teenagers and four sleepy chaperones attended worship together on Sunday morning.

It was a sad day when we learned that one of our teenage friends at church was moving away. Everyone hated to see him go. We decided to have a party for him on the houseboat owned by the bank where my husband worked, and we ordered a large, decorated 'good luck' cake from the bakery to surprise the departing teenager.

We hid the cake in the houseboat, and carried on the rest of the food. It was a chilly day, as we left the docks, the teenagers were inside, outside, and on top of the boat. The sliding glass door to the front deck was opened, and closed, opened, and closed, depending on how cold the kids felt, and how often they chose to go in and out.

We anchored our houseboat in a cove and ate our picnic. Then it was time for the surprise. Several teenagers helped me get the cake out of the closet. We put it on the inside table while the going-away-teenager was outside on the front deck.

"I'll carry the cake out to him," my husband said. He picked up the cake, and walked to the doorway, shouting "Surprise!"

Everyone turned their heads to watch as he walked the cake INTO the closed sliding glass door.

The beautiful cake folded in half. Its icing 'frosted' the glass. My husband stopped and starred in shocked surprise.

There was total silence, as everyone looked at the cake, and realized what had happened.

Then I started to laugh. I couldn't help it. The stunned look on my husband's face; the slightly crushed cake; and the glass door frosted in white icing were the funniest things I had ever seen. My husband looked at me, and he started laughing, too.

Then the teenagers joined in. We laughed until we were out of breath, and tears rolled down our cheeks.

When we were finally able to contain our laughter, we cut the slightly crunched-up cake, and ate it. It was delicious. So was the laughter we shared all evening long.

It could have been a sad farewell. But dear old Dad made sure it wasn't. He crushed the cake and, because he knew how to laugh at himself, he became the unexpected 'life' of the party that day in May.

On Sunday mornings, the teenagers in our class often tried to talk us out of Bible lessons. They wanted to talk about cheating in class at school, or the latest movies they had seen instead. We listened to them talk for the first part of the hour, then we related the latest movies and the cheating to Bible teachings. Their thought-provoking discussions were lively, and spiritually uplifting.

I thought the teenagers who had gone to church school all their lives would know the Bible. But when it became apparent they didn't, we planned several six-week courses on people and events in the Bible. "First we'll take a quiz on a specific part of the Bible, then after we read and discuss that part, we'll take the Bible quiz again," I announced in class.

"We don't want to study the Bible," they said. "It's boring."

"Bear with me," I said with a smile. "I assure you, the Bible is NOT boring. You just need to get to know the people in it, and what God wanted them to do."

We worded the questions to make the teenagers curious: Who sent a beautiful woman's husband to die in battle so he could marry her? Who was the beautiful woman? What did God do about it?

Every teenager in class studied the Bible to find the answers. They talked about David and Bathsheba, and God's judgement on David, and David's shame.

At the end of the hour, we closed with David's lament in Psalms 51:1-4.

"But I thought David was a righteous man chosen by God," one of the teenagers said.

"God worked with the imperfect people who were living then" I replied. "Just as He works with you and me today."

At the end of the first six- week course, the teenagers voted to continue studying people in the Bible. They all agreed that reading about real people and their problems in Biblical times was definitely NOT boring.

Share the humor often. It reinforces harmony in our lives.

"What did Adam say on the day before Christmas?
"It's Christmas, Eve."

"What do you call it when batman skips church?"
"Christian Bale"

"Who was the greatest comedian in the Bible?"
"Samson. He brought the house down."

Be full of gratitude. Gratitude changes everything.

Be full of joy. Joy is the simplest form of gratitude.
Be full of faith. With faith all things are possible.
Be full of hope.   Hope lives in the hearts of those
who have faith.

Smile. Kindness and respect begin with a smile.

Share a smile. Save the world.

Made in the USA
Middletown, DE
01 November 2020